Ballinspittle:
Moving Statues and Faith

TIM RYAN
and
JUREK KIRAKOWSKI

THE MERCIER PRESS
CORK and DUBLIN

The Mercier Press Limited
4 Bridge Street, Cork
24 Lower Abbey Street, Dublin 1

ISBN 0-85342-758-5

The authors and publisher would like to thank the *Cork Examiner* and the *Evening Echo* for permission to use their photographs and *Phoenix* magazine for permission to use the cartoons on page 70.

Contents

Introduction

'Oh look! She's Moving!'

In July of 1985, seven people from the parish of Ballinspittle in south-west Cork were passing the Marian shrine at Sheehy's Cross during their nightly stroll. They stopped, as many Irish people would, to offer a decade of the rosary at the shrine. Then a strange occurrence took place, the reverberations and implications of which were to set in motion a chain reaction that was eventually to amaze the world.

The statue of Our Lady appeared to move.

Very soon the shrine at Ballinspittle was inundated with pilgrims and the simply curious. At first they came from Cork, twenty-five miles of rural roads away. Then the news spread. CIE, the national transport service, began a regular bus service to the shrine. Folk came from other parts of the country, from Dublin. Buses came from London. The media arrived. There was scarcely a night in this hitherto-unknown rural hamlet during which some television crew or other were not filming the goings-on.

The village folk were at their wits' end in trying to cope with this undreamt-of onrush. A committee was set up; stewards were drafted in from neighbouring parishes; the garda síochána sent reinforcements to the local station to help with the traffic problem.

Soon word came of sightings and apparitions in other parts of the country, in Leinster and Connaught. A new phenomenon was in the making. Pundits gave conflicting opinions; scientists ran to their textbooks; priests to their bishops. The letters columns of the national newspapers bulged with eyewitness accounts and personal experiences.

The two authors of this book have been involved with the phenomenon since the first sightings. Tim Ryan is a reporter with the national daily newspaper, the *Cork Examiner*, and Dr Jurek Kirakowski is a lecturer in psychology at University College, Cork. The purpose in writing this book is twofold. Firstly, many people are looking for an overview of what happened during the summer of 1985, and the authors believe that the many eye-witness accounts they have cited form a unique historical document. Secondly, many people have looked for an explanation, and have been bemused by the many conflicting opinions that have been set forth. The authors tried to do justice to all, in an objective and rational way, without being one-sided (although it is fair to say they do have their own views on the matter).

There are two parts in this book. In the first three chapters, Tim Ryan outlines the background to the shrine, the first and subsequent eye-witness testimonies, and the multiplication of parallel claims that followed. In chapters 4, 5 and 6, Dr Kirakowski outlines the psychological investigations he and his team of researchers made of the Ballinspittle phenomenon, and then goes on to consider the wider personal, scientific and social implications. In the Epilogue, an account is given of the Catholic Church's viewpoint on the matter.

It is important that the 'Ballinspittle phenomenon' is not brushed under the carpet or ignored as a five-day wonder. The implications for the future are vast and are only now beginning to emerge. The authors hope that this book will provide basic documentation about the origins and implications of what began in the tiny village of Ballinspittle in the summer of 1985.

The people who have helped us during the compilation of this book are too numerous to mention in a short introduction: you will see their names cropping up again and again in the subsequent chapters. To each one of them, we wish to express a sincere thanks and hope that our work has not misrepresented their valuable contributions.

Tim Ryan & Jurek Kirakowski
Cork, October 1985

Claire O'Mahony – the first person to see movements of the statue at Ballinspittle

Photo : Eddie O'Hare

Hundreds pray before 'moving' statue

By JIM CLUSKEY

HUNDREDS of people gathered in fog and rain last night to pray and sing hymns before a "moving" statue of the Blessed Virgin near a small West Cork village.

The first movements of the statue in a hillside grotto near Ballinspittle were noticed on Monday at 10 p.m. by two women who had stopped to pray.

The word of their experience soon spread and throughout Tuesday and into the early hours of yesterday morning, people streamed to the grotto to watch and pray.

Almost all those who saw the statue move were reluctant to talk about their experience.

However, two young men, Kevin Hannon (23) and Gerard O'Donovan (17) told the *Examiner* they were absolutely positive they had seen a movement of the head and shoulders at about 11.45 on Tuesday night.

Kevin, who was watching the statue — about 30 feet up a hillside — through binoculars, said the movement was "to and fro." Both said the experience was "something of a shock."

A lady in her twenties who didn't want to be named also confirmed that she had seen movements of the statue.

"My impression was that the shoulders were swaying from side to side," she said.

"Others who saw it said there was a backward and forward movement of the head and nearly everyone who saw it said the statue was shivering or moving.

"One woman thought she saw the face of Our Lord coming into the face of the Virgin."

Last night at about 10 o'clock a woman collapsed in a faint in front of the shrine and was carried away moaning and crying. It was believed she had been overcome by the tangible emotion of the occasion.

The shrine was created by local voluntary workers some 30 years ago at the instigation of local publican Mr. Robert Nash. The statue of the Virgin and another of St. Bernadette were purchased with local subscriptions.

The first report of the 'moving' statue at Ballinspittle which appeared in the CORK EXAMINER on 25th July, 1985.

A photograph of the crowd after the first movements on 22 July.

This photograph was taken on 24 July by Eddie O'Hare

1: A Small Shrine in the Country

Ballinspittle is a small rural village situated some twenty-five miles south-west of Cork city. Though only a few miles from the picturesque fishing village of Kinsale it was previously unknown to most outsiders except those tourists who chanced to stray into it while touring the Old Head of Kinsale area. Like many another Irish village, stories as to the origin of its name abound in the locality. Its name in Irish is Béal Átha 'n Spidéal meaning the mouth of the ford of the hospital. Locals claim that a hospital was located in olden days on a site near the village church. The Church of the Holy Trinity in Ballinspittle is claimed to be the oldest in the diocese of Cork. The parish is joined with neighbouring Ballinadee for administrative purposes and both are currently served by only one priest, though this is a recent development.

The present grotto at Ballinspittle is located within a half mile of the village in the townland of Dromdough, translated from the Irish 'the Dewy's Hill'. The idea to build a grotto at all was first mentioned in 1954, the Marian year. The suggestion was a simple one – to do something to mark the Marian year as was happening in virtually every parish throughout Ireland. The suggestion was considered and the matter was referred to the parish committee. In February the parish committee decided to send a deputation consisting of John O'Donovan, Billy Quinn of Kilcoleman and Denis O'Reilly of Kilgobbin to the local priest Fr McCarthy to ask his permission for the erection of a grotto. This request was readily granted.

Next was the choosing of a location and a number of sites were inspected during the spring of 1954. In this regard local publican Robert Nash was of great assistance. A site near the holy well at Kilbrittain was considered as was the quarry site, now a carpark near Ballinspittle. In the end the present location was chosen primarily because of the natural rockface of the site. The land was donated by a local farmer, Denis O'Leary of Dromdough, known locally as Din Leary. However before any statue could be erected a lot of basic work had to be done. This was undertaken by an ad hoc committee set up and virtually every local man capable of hard physical labour came to the site each night at 8 pm. Even in 1954 there were three tractors in the parish and all were used in the gathering of materials. Bushes and rough vegetation were cut away, the water was drained off and deep crevices were filled in. Some of the crevices between the grotto and the road were ten to twelve feet deep, Denis O'Reilly recalls. Men who toiled hard at the time and who are still active on the new committee include Stephen Nolan, Denis O'Reilly, Miah O'Reilly, John O'Donovan, Michael O'Reilly, Robert Collins and Joe Hayes.

The shape and size of the statue itself had next to be decided on and in the end a model, based on Lourdes, which also included a smaller statue of St Bernadette was chosen. Both statues were donated. The statues were moulded at Bernardi's of Paul Street, Cork City, by Maurice O'Donnell who now lives in Gurranabraher in the northern part of the city. Today he is Ireland's only statue maker and carries on his own business in a yard in Coach Street. 'There was nothing special about that one,' he recalls. 'I remember it going out. It is exactly the same as the one in the grotto in Glanmire, they were both based on a French model.' The five foot six inches statue of Our Lady was set in solid concrete. Having been allowed to dry it was covered with soft plaster and then, as was normal procedure, rubbed down with sandpaper. In all it took about three weeks to make both statues for Ballinspittle. Some years ago,due probably to the changes brought in by Vatican II, demand for statues lessened and Bernardi's closed their premises. Maurice managed to retrieve some of the old moulds for his own use but unfortunately the one for the Ballinspittle statue was lost.

The day before the official opening took place the fire brigade arrived and washed down the area making everything clean and tidy for the big day.

The official opening took place on 8 December 1954. The blessing was performed by the curate Fr Jack Murphy in front of a large attendance. In the early years there was always an annual procession to the grotto from the village church and back again but this was dropped in recent years due to the pressure of traffic. However the rosary continued to be recited all during the month of May each year and on 15 August, the feast of the Assumption.

The first reports of the statue in the grotto at Ballinspittle 'moving' go back at least fifteen years. At that time according to locals two priests claimed to have seen strange 'movements' at the shrine as they prayed. In 1981 two local children claim to have seen it 'move'. On 15 August 1982 a cousin of Mrs O'Mahony, one of the seven people who saw the movement on 22 July, claimed that Our Lady 'blinked' as she prayed. In 1983 two of Mrs O'Mahony's own children claimed to have seen it 'move'. Their mother simply told them to go away and 'have their eyes tested'. And there are numerous other reports.

The 22 July 1985 was the feast day of Mary Magdalene. On the evening of that day Mrs Pat Daly of Dromdough thought it would be a nice idea for her husband Christopher and herself to go for a walk by the shrine. The Dalys are natives to the area. Christopher works locally in the boat yard at Kilmacsimon near Innishannon. They describe themselves as very ordinary people and not over religious. They go to Mass every Sunday but rarely make it during the week, they readily admit. On the evening of 22 July they were joined for their walk by their two young sons John aged ten and Michael aged seven. Mrs Daly decided to invite along their next door neighbour, Mrs O'Mahony, for company.

Mrs Catherine O'Mahony is a widow. Originally from Dunderrow across the Bandon river she has lived all her married life in Dromdough. Mrs O'Mahony also regards herself as a very average Catholic but admits that she has prayed more since her husband died. She was the woman who back in 1983 had laughed at the idea when her children told her they had seen the statue 'move'.

Pat Daly takes up the story: 'We decided to go for a walk, so we dressed up and called up next door for Mrs O'Mahoney. "I'm very tired, I'm not going at all tonight," said Mrs O'Mahony.

"Come on, dress up," I said, and she did.' Eventually the party of seven set out – Christopher and Pat Daly with their sons John and Michael with Mrs Catherine O'Mahony, and her daughters Helen (twelve) and Claire (seventeen).

'It was half past nine when we arrived at Sheehy's Cross and I said we would go as far as the grotto. We were struggling along looking at this and that and as we were passing the grotto Mrs O'Mahony suggested that we would say one decade of the rosary. So we knelt down and we were almost finished the decade and the next thing Claire says to John in a whisper, "The grotto is moving. See."

'"Stop it," I said.

'We had our decade finished and the next thing John said to me: "Mammy, the grotto is moving mad."

'"God knows 'tis," said Mrs O'Mahony.

'So we were all there looking and and saying: "Jeepers God, what's happening at all?"

'Mrs O'Mahony said we should finish the rosary. So we finished our prayers and the movements to and fro continued. We were not afraid but we knew it was not normal. It was now about 10.10 pm and we said we would ring up for John O'Donovan who was always in charge of the grotto. He might know if anyone had reported the movement before. He was away on holidays as it happened but his son came down and a few more as well. We stopped the passers-by. We didn't tell them what we saw but they too said: "Oh Look, she's moving from the shoulders up." They all had different experiences. We said another rosary and before the night was finished we had thirteen people in all gathered there. Finally we left for home at around 12.40 am.'

Seventeen-year-old Claire O'Mahony was the first person to see the statue 'move'. She is a student at the Vocational

School in Kinsale and at the time was about to enter Leaving Certificate class. 'When we finished the rosary I looked up and I saw her move. I said this is my imagination. Then John Daly came over to me and I asked him did it move and he said it did. And when the rosary had finished I told my mum. She saw it too. We saw it all that night. The statue moved backwards and forwards as if she were breathing.'

Claire has been to the shrine several times since 22 July but has not seen any further movement. She has drawn no conclusions whatever about her observations and retains an entirely open mind.

Christopher Daly's account is similar. 'I saw it myself, the movement backwards and forwards.' Later the then curate of Ballinspittle asked him what exactly he saw. 'He questioned me in some detail and said he would keep an open mind on the matter.' Mr Daly and some locals went right up to the statue and examined it to see how it was set. 'I found it was fixed solid in a cement base.'

The head of the statue of Our Lady is surrounded by a halo of bulbs which are automatically lit from 10 pm to 2.20 am. On the night of 22 July a garda patrol car arrived very late, when the lights had in fact been switched off. The garda car shone its spotlight on the statue and according to Mr Daly 'thirty out of the fifty people then present saw the movement.'

John Daly is a fifth class pupil in Ballinspittle National School. John was the second person to see the statue 'move'. 'The lights in the centre of the halo over her head went off,' he claims. 'They went off and came on again three times. The statue moved sideways and then it was moving forwards and back. At times you think like that it was going to fall out.' Most of his classmates saw it move as well, he claims. In fact one of his pals, Paul McCarthy saw Our Lord's face on the statue. When he returned to school after the summer holidays his teacher asked him to tell the story to the class. But he doesn't really know what his teacher thinks of it, he hasn't told John. 'Loads of newspaper people have asked me questions though,' says John.

Mrs Catherine O'Mahony's story bears out the evidence of the other six. 'We were saying the rosary and herself (Claire) and John Daly were doing the fool. I was taking no notice of them at all and then when the decade of the rosary was finished John said: "The statue is moving". After a while I saw it moving. It seemed to me as if she was breathing. Breathing or sighing. 'Twas chest movements I saw from the waist up.'

One thing is common to all seven of the original witnesses, they have seen very little if any signs of movement since. This they explain by the fact that they became very involved in organising and stewarding of the crowds who suddenly began to descend on the grotto. Some six weeks later, however, on a wet night Mrs O'Mahony saw our Lady 'touch her head off her left shoulder and then a few nights later I saw her shimmer as a lake would'. Neither Mrs O'Mahony nor any of the six saw any hand movements or transformations of the face.

All the original witnesses are very frank in their testimony and do not attach any particular significance to it apart from the unusual happening that the statue appeared to 'move'. Mrs O'Mahony wonders how people can see the faces of various saints on the statue since people do not really know what these people looked like when they lived, thousands of years ago in most cases. She argues, for example that Our Lady looked like an Egyptian and the closest figure she has seen is in the Basilica in Lourdes.

The lives of the seven have not altered very much since 22 July. For the younger folk it was simply back to school again and the humdrum of homework and school life. The adults still give a helping hand with the organising of the stewarding but none are in the newly set-up supervising committee, by choice. They admit that they are probably more religiously aware nowadays. 'Before I used to simply go round the beads each night,' says Mrs Catherine O'Mahony, 'but now I find that I meditate more on the mysteries and on what lies behind the decades. I think that is a good thing.' But none of them can explain why this has happened in Ballinspittle – or in some thirty other venues throughout Ireland.

One of the remarkable things about the Ballinspittle phenomenon was the rapidity with which the crowds began to assemble. This was due largely to the fact that the majority of visitors could see the movement for themselves with their own eyes. John Murray, a garda sergeant based at McCurtain Street in Cork city was the first to give public witness to the happenings. His testimony added greatly to the credibility and increased the attention of the public.

On Wednesday, 24 July, two days after the first reports, he visited the shrine. He had, he said, been very sceptical about reports of the 'moving' statue which had been circulating since Monday. 'I arrived at the grotto at about half past nine,' he told the *Cork Examiner*, 'and at exactly 10.06 the head and shoulders of the Blessed Virgin moved to and fro to such an extent that I thought it would topple over. It also vibrated from side to side as if someone was pushing it. Lots of people were there and saw the same thing.' On the following morning on his way to work Sergeant Murray, like Christopher Daly, checked the base of the statue and found it – solid concrete.

Another local girl, Mary O'Sullivan (seventeen) of Garretstown told of how she along with her mother and five brothers witnessed the miraculous movements on 24 July: 'About 3.30am in the morning, when most of the others had gone away Our Lady opened her hands. We put on the lamp which we pointed on the statue and again we saw the movement. We and a few others remained on and said the rosary.'

The *Cork Examiner* contacted the local parish priest Fr Donal Neville for reaction. He had 'no comment' to make on the reports and had certainly not seen the statue 'move' himself.

Within days thousands were flocking to Ballinspittle to see the 'moving' statue. On the night of 26 July an estimated 3,000 people descended on an unprepared village. An ad hoc committee of stewards was hard pressed to control the traffic. They were lucky in that the grotto is conveniently located on one side of a triangular road network. From 9 pm each night a stream of traffic came from all sides and by 10 pm the area in and around the grotto was a mass of people. Soon the reports of 'movement' would move through the crowd and upwards of seventy per cent of those present were satisfied that they had witnessed a supernatural happening.

John Hayes, a civil engineer, travelled from Tipperary on 26 July to examine the surroundings. 'It definitely appears to move,' he concluded, 'but I am satisfied that it is an optical illusion because of the quivering of one's eyes while focusing on a bright object at that range.'

On 27 July Eric Treacy, a restauranteur from Douglas outside Cork city drove to Ballinspittle 'out of curiosity'. He was greatly shocked by what he saw and 'just could not understand it'.

The crowds continued to grow. The stewards erected barriers of rope and directed the 'pilgrims' into a natural amphitheatre on the opposite side of the road. The rosary was recited constantly over a loud-hailer system. The atmosphere each night was remarkably peaceful. By 1 August reports of complete transformations of the statue were reported. It seemed as if the entire litany of saints had chosen to make themselves visible at Ballinspittle. Naoimh O'Sullivan from Bandon was one enthusiastic viewer: 'Sometimes it's the face of Our Lord I see but if you look a second time it's back to Our Lady again.'

Sean Walsh from Cloghagh, Co. Cork had a similar mystical experience: 'I was up at the altar praying. Suddenly this blackness came over the face, it was man-like. It was really amazing.'

One of the more extraordinary stories came from Mrs Kathleen O'Dwyer of Carrigaline Road in Douglas. She visited the shrine on Saturday night, 27 July and saw the statue 'move'. Then on Sunday as she ate her dinner she noticed a rose blooming in the garden and decided to take it to the shrine. Along with her husband, son and some friends she arrived in Ballinspittle at 4.30 pm. As they talked she suddenly noticed the hands of Our Lady open and her beads spread. Meanwhile her husband and son saw the face of Our Lady transformed into that of Our Lord. All were stunned and astonished.

Local man Denis O'Reilly, a member of the original committee in 1954 and now a Fine Gael county councillor saw the movement on 27 July. 'At 10.05 pm I saw it sway from right to left and again on 31 July when the halo was gone out early in the morning I saw the hands part and the rose illuminate.'

By this time the committee were putting together accounts of the various reports. Those named agreed to allow their evidence to be used in any investigation.

One witness is a young mother, Claire O'Loughlin from Greenmount. Her entry reads: '5.20 pm, 8 August 1985. Came Sunday afternoon. Thought an image of Our Lord was present. Today a man's figure, full beard and long hair towered over Our Lady. Thought this man to be Our Lord. Both had a halo. Both halos similar. Prepared to testify.'

Neither were foreigners blind to the movements. Elisa Mucedere from Italy but now living in Terenure in Dublin on 7 August saw 'the face of Jesus of Nazareth as he entered Jerusalem on Palm Sunday.' Another Italian, Maria Alicandi had exactly the same experience. Three carloads of Wexford people had also seen changes in the face of the statue. They had seen 'her right hand move along the left one'. When asked how they could be so certain of what they had seen, they replied that there were 'little blue bands at the end of Our Lady's habit' which they saw come closer together.

By the end of the first week of August the area around the shrine had taken on the appearance of a permanent place of pilgrimage. Two new telephone kiosks were discreetly installed at the base of the hill near the grotto and foundations had been laid for toilets. Representations led by local councillor Denis O'Reilly were making regular trips to officials in County Hall seeking a large scale grant for the widening of roads and the provision of public lighting.

Among the early visitors to the grotto were members of the media and this is the subject of a later chapter. On Friday 2 August Dublin journalist Kevin D. O'Connor arrived in Ballinspittle at the request of the RTÉ *Pat Kenny Show*. The producer had sent him down bcause he could be relied upon to be 'objective'. In the *Irish Independent* of 21 August he wrote:

> . . .After a while I felt slowly suffused with pleasure, just watching. The features went out of focus and when they resumed the hands were up to the side of the face, as if she had received a blow. I felt tears come into my eyes at the hurt she was undergoing. She seemed to be passively suffering this pain without protest. In a kind of trance, but aware of what I was doing I leaned across to a person next to me and asked if they had seen the movement. "No," the girl said. . . There is no rule about it. Some of the pious don't see. Some of the sceptical do. . . The very uptight and totally resistant probably would not. . . All sorts of things go on in this life that puzzle me and leave me without explanation.'

While no serious disturbances of any consequence took place at the grotto the hastily put together committee did an excellent job in the early days of great pressure. The numbers on the committee of stewards quickly reached the one hundred mark. Several of the surrounding parishes offered their help and assisted in any way they could. The garda station at Ballinspittle has only two full-time men and these were augmented with reinforcements from the Bandon traffic corps. The traffic problems remained the largest headache for the committee but the increasing number of buses rather than cars alleviated the crisis to some extent. Buses were parked in large open areas at Barrell's Cross and in the village square. From the first week of reports of 'movement' the immediate roads close to the grotto were entirely sealed off from traffic and from that time on there were no major traffic jams.

Many remarked on the peaceful atmosphere at the shrine. However, for many, emotions were high and some experienced stress. On 30 August Michael Fehilly of Ballycattan, Kilbrittain collapsed and died on the hill opposite the shrine. A doctor who was in the crowd was on hand within minutes as were the Red Cross who maintained a nightly presence in Ballinspittle.

As 15 August, the feast of the Assumption, approached, the

largest number of pilgrims ever were expected in Ballinspittle. Words of caution uttered by the Bishop of Cork and Ross, Dr Michael Murphy had little effect. 'Direct supernatural intervention is,' said Bishop Murphy, 'a very rare happening in life, so commonsense would demand that we approach the claims made concerning the grotto at Ballinspittle with prudence and caution.'

CIE advertised the laying on of special bus services throughout the afternoon of 15 August from both Cork city centre and surrounding towns. In Ballinspittle on the night of 14 August a special meeting of all parishoners and stewards was held at the grotto to finalise details. Some members of the committee had discussions with Bandon gardaí to work out the traffic arrangements. From early morning all roads within a mile of the shrine would be sealed off and pilgrims were advised to come well clad. No hawkers of any kind were allowed in line with the committee's view that no commercial streak would be tolerated. Chip vans had to be content to park in the village square where, nevertheless, business was brisk. The hours between 2 pm and 4 pm were set aside specially for the handicapped and the elderly who were allowed up close to the railings. Meanwhile back in Cork city Bishop Murphy was making preparations to celebrate the annual diocesan mass at a shrine on the Lee Road. The faithful in Cork were urged to attend this mass. The Bishop had earlier refused a request by the committee for the celebration of mass at Ballinspittle though permission had been granted in 1984. The committee accepted the rejection quietly and without comment.

On Thursday, 15 August, the feastday of the Assumption, devotions at the shrine began at 12 noon and continued until the early hours of Friday morning. In all some sixty rosaries were recited in addition to hymn singing. A new car park was opened in a nearby disused quarry and the county council had piped the stream that flows opposite the grotto. Efforts to have toilet facilities ready in time failed.

Estimates by gardaí put the crowd in excess of 15,000. It was described by committee chairman Brendan Murphy as 'by far the biggest to date'. Though the expected thousands did not materialise during the day, nightfall drew thousands from all the approach roads. For those who had not been to the shrine for some days the scene had been completely transformed. The gentle stream which once flowed by the road side had now been piped and what was once a green field had become a giant brown amphitheatre. The stewards, clad in brightly coloured markings kept strict order while the ladies' committee made very welcome refreshing cups of tea. Among the visitors was Our Lady of Lourdes Choir from Ballinlough and the Riverstick Folk Group. Both were warmly received by the crowd. Each rosary was dedicated to a special cause – to people awaiting examination results, to people seriously ill and 'to those no longer with us who helped build this shrine.' Most who had come for the night brought baskets of food and enjoyed a mini-picnic high on the hillside while the more fervent grasped their rosary beads and stared harder to see the wonderful 'movement'. A Church of Ireland farmer, Christopher Draper, who was helping with the stewarding spoke to the *Cork Examiner* of his experiences: 'I saw a shaking from the shoulders up,' he said, 'but I have not seen it by daylight and I stress that. My wife has seen it and so have some of the kids. I was very sceptical when I saw it first but you can't say your own eyes are telling lies.'

Teresa O'Donnell of Toureen, Skibbereen told of a more remarkable experience. On 25 July she and her family came to the shrine and saw the statue appear to grow larger and clearer. In the following night she saw 'a small silver cross shining very brightly' on a nearby hill which others saw but which in reality was not there at all. 'It was shining very brightly,' said Teresa. 'I assumed it had always been there.' Up on the hillside a group of ladies from Seamus Murphy Place in Mallow agreed that they had certainly seen the statue 'move' but two elderly gentlemen from Fermoy completely failed to see anything at all. 'We're not sure, it's hard to say,' said one of a group of Bavarians sitting high on the hill. 'It could be the lights.' They were not impressed and would not be coming back again.

The committee had been successful in keeping the area non-commercial. Chippers and hawkers were confined to the village while over in nearby Garrettstown the Atlantic Hotel remained open until the early hours to cater for the late night travellers. One enterprising young lady was selling 'postcards of Our Lady of Ballinspittle sketched by an artist at the shrine today'. She was doing very well, she reported. As midnight approached committee chairman Brendan Murphy was still working hard supervising his stewards. Over the loud hailer system he said he wished to thank everybody who helped in any way. He regretted that earlier some stewards had a 'brush-in' with people from the multi-channel company in Cork who arrived 'with not a very nice attitude'.

'And what of the future?' asked a reporter.

'In a week's time we will sit down and look back on what has happened,' he replied. 'Then we will try to plan ahead. As far as we are concerned we have a place of pilgrimage here, probably forever.'

It was hard to disagree with him.

The media were present in large numbers on 15 August and all carried lengthy reports the following morning. However, not everyone was enthusiastic. On the night of 15 August United Press International in its worldwide dispatch issued a comment from the head of Ireland's Government Information Service, Mr Peter Prendergast. Mr Prendergast was quoted as saying 'three-quarters of the world is laughing heartily' at the Ballinspittle happenings.

The Press Secretary refused to say, however, if the remark attributed to him reflected his thinking on the 'moving' statue. When asked for his opinion he replied: 'I have nothing further to say.' When again contacted by the *Examiner* some weeks later he commented: 'At least it made a great August story.'

With the passing of the feast of the Assumption the numbers journeying to Ballinspittle decreased to a more steady and consistent turn out. Large buses from virtually every part of the country replaced the cars by and large as most of the local Cork people had by now paid at least one visit. Though strongly encouraged by the local committee to do otherwise the pilgrims continued to make the journey at night time to attain the best view of the 'magic' statue. In the aftermath of 15 August weekend nights saw upwards of fifty buses parked at Barrell's Cross and in the village.

During the last week of August rumours of the first miraculous cure at Ballinspittle were rife. A lady suffering from arthritis had reportedly abandoned her crutches at the grotto but nothing could be confirmed. Then in the second week of September the local committee called a press conference and presented evidence of the first 'miracle'. A young housewife, Mrs Frances O'Riordain, aged thirty-six, from the north side of Cork city, who had been completely deaf since she was twenty, claimed that she had had her hearing restored during a visit to Ballinspittle. Mrs O'Riordain suffered an attack of measles when she was four years old and over the following seventeen years her hearing gradually diminished until at twenty she was 'stone deaf'. On 31 July along with her husband Noel and sister-in-law, she visited Ballinspittle. Standing on the hillside Frances experienced the 'movement' in the statue. 'My body felt as though it was exploding and I thought I was going to choke – and then I heard it – the crowd singing and *Ave Maria* were the first words I heard. I told my sister-in-law and she knew I couldn't be lip-reading because it was so dark. She just said, "Take it easy, take your time." I was terribly excited,' said Mrs O'Riordain, 'but I told nobody about the incident.' Later the family decided to tell the committee. Mrs O'Riordain had been recently fitted with a hearing aid and was told how she now had 'nearly 30% hearing' by her doctor who, however, has said he will not comment for twelve months. Three years ago she claims she went to an eminent ear specalist at a Cork hospital with a view to having an operation but was told there was nothing the medics could do as both ear drums were permanently damaged. 'I went to the local priest and he said to wait twelve months before doing anything, but I'd go to the Pope in Rome if he wanted to see for himself. I firmly believe I was cured in Ballinspittle.'

2: In the Eyes of the World

The very first report of a 'moving' statue at Ballinspittle was written in the *Cork Examiner* issue of 24 July by reporter Jim Cluskey. 'Hundreds of people gathered in fog and rain last night to pray and sing hymns before a "moving" statue of the Blessed Virgin near a small west Cork village,' he wrote. The report also told of how 'at about 10 o'clock a woman collapsed in a faint in front of the shrine and was carried away moaning and crying. It was believed she has been overcome by the tangible emotion of the occasion'.

Soon letters poured into the newspaper. In the *Examiner* of 28 August Mrs Eileen Lynch of Coachford, Co. Cork wrote:

> I visited the grotto in Ballinspittle. . . It was my first visit there. I was very impressed by the secluded area woven by nature into a little heavenly venue. The stars on the statue in lieu of the usual plain crown, told their own tale and, as I looked at it for approximately ten minutes I saw nothing but I heard the surrounding crowd remark the movements.
>
> The public rosary started. At the end of the third decade I was amazed that I should see the statue move. I went closer and could see it better; it seemed actually to vibrate. Praise be to God was all I could say. Could a grief stricken mother do more to call her children from sin to save their immortal souls?
>
> The rejection of the Blessed Virgin by the atheist mods of today may well be why the woman who will crush the head of the serpent is giving us a sign to strengthen our faith.

Miss S. Murray of Macroom wrote:

> Seeing and hearing about Ballinspittle I decided to write.

> I was there twice – on 9 and 15 August. I saw the statue of Our Lady moving. The first time the halo flickered, then moved from side to side and finally the face of Jesus appeared. The second time the halo was brighter, the movement from side to side first and then backwards and forwards. The hands came apart after that and then the cloak moved.
>
> I hope that it will become a place of public prayer like Knock and Lourdes. It's a pity that there wasn't mass there on the Feast Day of the Assumption.

A letter headed 'Time to speak Out' was written by Padraig O'Siochain of Enniskeane, Co. Cork:

> In the light of recent and current events in West Cork it would surely seem obvious that the greatest and most needed miracle that Our Blessed Lady, the Mother of God, could perform for us would be to restore to us the moral courage of our forefathers so that we speak out against and reject the flood of foreign filth and immorality that is smothering Ireland today.
>
> Where, oh where, are the shepherds of the scattering flock? The silence is deafening! Surely it is time they stopped looking for reds under the bed and face up to the real enemies of society and of Ireland!

Such letters and nationwide interest in the new phenomenon drew some of the best known newspaper columnists and reporters to Ballinspittle.

T. P. O'Mahony, the Religious Affairs correspondent of the *Irish Press* who visited Ballinspittle put forward his viewpoint in an article on 27 August. He wrote:

> . . . Personally I find what has been 'happening' there very disturbing. Others have had very different kinds of reaction. I have spoken to many of them and I can of course (and do) respect that without subscribing to it. I can also be frightened by it.
>
> It's the numbers that bother me. On an individual basis

> I have no difficulty at all coping with the notion that someone finds it helpful to go and pray at a grotto in Ballinspittle. But I start worrying when 15,000 or 20,000 people turn up there amid mind-boggling reports of statue 'movements'. What are they looking for? Is it some kind of collective neurosis at work here? I'll settle for saying that the phenomenon is now bordering on the superstitious, bearing in mind that it is a mark of the superstitious personality that he or she looks outside him/herself for a solution to problems.
>
> The flight to Ballinspittle, in others words, is a flight from self-reliance, an exercise in unwillingness – an unwillingness to face our problem and work out our own solutions. The more we crave 'supernatural' re-assurance the less likely we are to confront our problems head on. Subconsciously we want an outside 'power' to intervene, to take over.
>
> Just this once (and only in relation to Ballinspittle, let me hasten to add) I'm inclined to follow the example of the great Spanish film director, Luis Brunuel, and say: 'I'm an atheist, thank God!'

The psychologists were already at work, too, putting their interpretations on events. (The second section of this book deals with this in great detail). In the same issue of the *Irish Press* (27 August), Dr Anthony Clare, a Dublin-born professor of psychiatry at St Bartholomew's Hospital in London offered his opinions:

> Most of the reports such as Our Lady's eyes moving are very difficult to establish, and they are easy to understand as possible tricks of the light transformed into fact by an intense desire to believe that something is happening. The sighting in Ballinspittle occurs late in the evening to women of great religious devotion.
>
> There is, of course, no way either a miracle or autosuggestion can be proved but the previous reports of statue movements from Asdee and Ballydesmond, the intense

> devotion and desire to believe of the women involved, the gloomy light and the powerful aura of an evening grotto together make a less supernatural explanation more than likely.
>
> Does it greatly matter one way or the other?
>
> There will be those, and I confess to be one of them, who find the spectacle of people waiting around for a special message something demeaning, as if God was just the latest of a long line of distinguished subscribers to Telecom Éireann. On the other hand, few unrealistic expectations have been raised.
>
> One of the women at Ballinspittle, for example, simply believed that the statue movement she had witnessed brought a silent message to people that it was time to pray, and the mass devotion that had subsequently been inspired does seem to be for the most part, beneficial.
>
> However, the spate of such reports suggests an intense need for a more simple, even infantile model of religious beliefs. Perhaps, it is said, the events and turmoil of contemporary Ireland, the sad saga of the Kerry babies, the steady toil of Northern Ireland, have induced an intense need to return to a much less complex world in which, like children, we wait expectantly for a reassuring message that God is with us, and will see us through our problems. In that sense, the psychological significance of the sightings is of as much interest as their spiritual significance. So many people reading so much significance into such banal events – statues moving their limbs, eyes, their clothes, suggests a very deep need, indeed, for simple re-assurance.

The notion that people are searching for something that is not being given to them, that the Catholic Church is lacking in some way is a recurring one. For the Church leaders the message seems abundantly clear.

The rapidity with which the phenomenon caught the attention of the national and international media was quite astonishing. Reference has already been made to Peter Prendergast's theory 'It made a great August story' but there was much more to it than just that. In the late days of July and early August there was rarely a night when some television crew or other were not filming. The British and foreign press moved in too in large numbers. Not all the reporters were very complimentary.

'A Moving Experience Comes to Ballinspittle Where They're Running Out of Space and Guinness' was how the *Daily Mail* headed their story of 3 August. Reporter John Edwards had been to Ireland to see 'the rocking Madonna of Co. Cork':

> After yesterday's meeting of the Ballinspittle Grotto Committee, chairman Brendan Murphy, puff-eyed with a terrible tiredness, said that if someone was sending the village a message he should have checked the facilities first. . . These happenings concerned the statue of the Virgin Mary which had stood in peace for thirty-one years in an ivy-covered cave in the hillside at Sand Cross.
>
> But when she was taking the air the other night, Clare Mahony, 17, looked up at the statue and said the whole 3 cwt. of it was 'rocking towards me.'
>
> Just a whisper of something like this in Ireland is the same as taking two minutes of prime time television.
>
> There have been no miracles. Just a death. A man had a heart attack climbing up on the top of Michael McCarthy's field to look down on the masses. . .
>
> So yesterday, with as he said, people falling out of the heaven on them, Brendan Murphy called for help. Later a bulldozer and people from the army turned up.
>
> Up the road at the grotto, one of the ladies on the committee said she had made notes of many sightings.
>
> 'The statue had been seen to wave its hand and also shake a foot,' she said.
>
> All this surprised Mr Nash (a local publican) who never heard of concrete performing like this before.
>
> 'Maybe it's something to do with the new radar station

at Ballydehob,' he said at lunchtime while waiting for the Guinness truck.

Even while the committee was meeting, someone ran in with news that a priest across in Courtmacsherry had a Virgin Mary statue which shook so much recently he had to hold on to it for an hour.

This was right in the middle of the Harbour Festival which welcomed the lift in a really dreadful season.

In late June 1985 Mayor Diane Feinstein of San Francisco arrived on a visit to Cork. The mayor and San Francisco were looked upon as a great hope for future investment in the city with high unemployment.

Dave Farrell, a reporter with the *San Francisco Chronicle* travelled with the huge contingent accompanying the mayor, and he wrote in the *Chronicle* on 27 July:

> Despite the adulation and publicity Feinstein is receiving, she has had to settle for smaller headlines than a statue of the Blessed Virgin Mary in a nearby village. At about the time Feinstein arrived, the Madonna, according to certain villagers, moved, quivered, shook, even walked. A thousand people crowded around the statue last night, knocking over a fence in their fervour.
>
> Although the common folk are rushing to see the miracle of the Madonna, the politicians are more interested in the monetary miracles that the saviour from San Francisco promises.
>
> They know, after all, that the Madonna never moves until after 10 at night, about the time the pubs close.

In the early days of August Gary Putka, a staff reporter with the *Wall Street Journal* came to spend some days in Cork, and Ballinspittle. On 15 August his two page report appeared in the European and American *Journal*.

> BALLINSPITTLE, Ireland – At twilight, when the crows fly to roost, people by the thousands flock to a nearby hillside in County Cork to pray before a statue of the Virgin Mary

in a grotto. Many of them say the statue moves. . . and in at least three other small towns in County Cork, people also insist that they have seen the inexplicable – Madonnas that blink and quiver, statues with vibrating halos and gesturing figures of Jesus. Church attendance is up, academics are issuing studies, offering scientific explanations and the first busloads of tourists are arriving. . . Many are just amused.

Asked how to get to Ballinspittle a Cork shopkeeper quips, 'Follow the star.' The *Cork Examiner* newspaper has carried several tongue-in-cheek references to the 'moving pole' in its coverage of a local traffic obstruction. One pilgrim, pointing to the sandwich trucks parked in Ballinspittle says, 'It's been a miracle for them, too.'

But apart from the sceptics' gibes runs a strain of something else – faint embarrassment about the Ireland that believes in divine intervention and 'signs' from heaven, that clings to a fundamentalist Roman Catholicism in a technocrat's world.

The Ireland of Ballinspittle is not the sophisticated, modern and youthful Ireland that the government has promised in its campaign to attract business investment in this depressed island, where unemployment averages 17%. 'We could probably do without something like this,' says one official at the Industrial Development Authority in Dublin. 'The image of Ireland that we want to project is not all this mass hysteria,' says Roy Johnston, a technology consultant in Dublin. 'Irish of any sensitivity are obviously ashamed by this nonsense, and it's not something you should be writing about. . .'

The Ballinspittle visions have put the church in an awkward spot – reluctant to dull people's devotion but unwilling to feed irrational behaviour. Bishop Murphy turned down a request for an Assumption day Mass at the grotto, although such a service was permitted last year. In a statement about the vision Bishop Murphy said mass prayer is a 'praiseworthy thing', but 'in instances of this kind, one has to be careful not to raise expectations unduly.'

On 26 August Ballinspittle's 'moving' statue could be said to have 'made it' in the news when *Time* magazine carried a short report under the heading 'Mysterious Lady.'

> Catherine O'Mahony and two of her children went out for their evening stroll near the Irish hamlet of B. . .
>
> Sceptics were very quick to brand the Ballinspittle Virgin as a case of mass hysteria or clever tourist promotion. Scientists from University College, Cork examined the statue, noted its setting 30 feet above eye level and its halo of blue electric lights and pronounced the entire effect an optical illusion. The finding had little effect on the believers. 'I think that God is sending us a sign to prepare us for the end of the world,' said Marie Costello, the local postmistress. Since Our Lady of Ballinspittle first began to move, residents of at least three other towns in the area have reported similar apparitions in local grottoes.

Meanwhile back at home the columnists were continuing to make the treck to West Cork. On 21 August Mary Holland devoted her column in the *Irish Times* to the happenings. Due to the inclement weather she had not been able to make the journey herself but had spoken to many who did. 'What has happened to them appears to have been a deeply moving religious experience and it is difficult to understand why it should have given rise to such hilarity,' she wrote.

In a particularly good analysis Ms Holland then broadened out her scope of enquiry:

> The message to the politicians is stark. For the yearning after old certainties goes beyond religious practice to reflect an unease with the quality of life in Ireland and with a society which, it now seems to many people, has failed them materially as well as spiritually.
>
> In many ways the shrine at Ballinspittle is the perfect symbol of post-Amendment Ireland. Prior to the Constitutional referendum of 1983, it still seemed that socio-

A group of people who have witnessed movement during daylight hours at Ballinspittle – (from left) Patrick Simms, Kathy O'Mahony, Maureen Moloney, Michael and Joseph Moore and Councillor Denis O'Reilly.

(Photo : Eddie O'Hare)

Members of the original 1954 Marian Year Grotto Committee

(Photo : Eddie O'Hare)

Photographs of the crowds taken on 15 August, the Feast of the Assumption

(photo : Eddie O'Hare)

political progress on a whole range of issues might evolve quite easily in this country, that we were becoming more tolerant, more open and generous in our willingness to discuss such issues as unwanted pregnancies, divorce, illegitimacy.

The Amendment changed that. At the time a lot of people said hopefully that it wouldn't have a long term effect, that it was a one-off experience which both sides wanted to put behind them. Since then we have had the the death of Ann Lovett. . . the Kerry Babies Tribunal. . . Jane O'Connor drowned in the River Dodder. . .

The Government is running scared on all these issues and,in a way, looking at all those faces at Ballinspittle, it's easy to understand why. Would you run a referendum on divorce, to take an issue at random, while the Virgin Mary was reminding them and thousands like them that Ireland had remained faithful to the Catholic Church through the worst of the penal days and occupied a special place in her heart?

On 27 August Ces Cassidy of the *Irish Independent* wrote an account of her trip on a bus from O'Connell Street Dublin to Ballinspittle. It's Saturday evening and 'the pilgrims settle in for the journey, some pulling out magazines, romantic books or copies of the New Testament. The bus holds a mixed bunch: mild-faced middle-aged couples, some elderly folk in their Sunday best, a couple of well-dressed young women in expensive casuals and a group of young girls in trendy jeans and tops.'

At 10 o'clock the bus approached the grotto:

About two miles from the grotto the first signs of commercialism show up, a burger stand and an ice-cream van on the roadside. It could be worse, if this was America the vendors would be selling 'Miracle Burgers' and 'Vigil Specials' and telling all the pilgrims to 'Have A Nice Pray.'

Ms Cassidy herself saw the movement but like any good

reporter remained quite rational:

> And indeed, staring at the statue with its dazzling bright halo, the figure of the Virgin gives the appearance of shimmering slightly.
>
> However, as the nearest anyone could get to the statue was 30 feet and the face of the concrete figure was being lit by at least a dozen flashlights from the crowd it is impossible to judge whether the pilgrims are seeing an actual phenomenon or merely an illusion of movement, created by the combination of the strong halo light with swaying bushes surrounding it, the distance, the darkness and the wind.
>
> What is certain is that an astonishing number of people present are reporting in tones of wonder a variety of sights.

On 8 August one of Ireland's most humorous and best loved columnists, Eanna Brophy of the *Sunday Press* visited Ballinspittle. Eanna does not leave us in suspense for in the second paragraph of his report he wrote: 'And yes, I did "see" some movement, and I did "see" the face seeming to change. But there were no miracles involved.' The significant thing about Eanna's comment is that he puts the inverted commas around the 'see' and not the 'movement', thereby apparently believing that the effect is caused by the witness and not by the statue. He continued:

> The halo of bulbs was throwing a deep shadow under the statue's chin. As I kept looking things began to blur a bit, and with a bit of imagination you could say that the shadow under the chin had become a beard. Various people have reported seeing the face of Christ or Padre Pio or St Joseph. And I could see why they would say this: the more I looked at the brightly lit statue, the more it became a strain on the eyes – and everyone else there was staring at it too. Naturally the effect of staring at a bright object set in dark background plays tricks with your eyes. All you need then is a bit of atmosphere and an eagerness to see strange things,

and you will.

I found that by tilting my head one way, I could see the 'bearded face', but a slight move of the head brought the statue back into proper focus. A young man beside me breathed 'She's moving well tonight!' I looked to see if he was joking but he wasn't: he looked quite excited. I moved in a bit nearer, and by staring for a long time, produced this effect on my own eyes. Then I looked up at the street lamp and got exactly the same result: the pole which held it began to waver back and forth. Eyestrain again.

Eanna Brophy's final conclusions entirely re-echo those of Mary Holland and T. P. O'Mahony.

The tales of Victor O'D Power held great sway over the Irish imagination in the days (and nights) before rural electrification and television. Today there are many who would like to return to the old certainties of those days, and who long for a sign or message of some kind that help is at hand. Add to this a bit of optical illusion and auto-suggestion and you have Ballinspittle.

The reporting team of the *Cork Examiner* kept a close eye on developments at Ballinspittle and in early September the night editorial staff visited the grotto to carry out a survey. Pat Casey reported on their findings in an article on 25 September. The group of six reporters were joined by four non-editorial employees, a teacher and a garda sergeant. Pat Casey wrote:

Any hope that any definite pattern might emerge from the observations of the participants was dashed on the return of the individual reports. Seven, including this writer, saw what appeared to the pronounced 'movement' of the statue. . . Only one of the group reported any spiritual or prayerful effect of the experience. . . Of the remaining group of five, four declared they observed a slight 'shimmering' but no 'movement'.

Only one of the group of twelve declared that she had

seen nothing at all. She questioned whether the recitation of the rosary was conducive to objective assessment!

Hotpress magazine reported on the happenings at Ballinspittle in its own inimitable style – and much to the chagrin of the local committee:

> Since then (22 July) there has been no rest for the people of Ballinspittle – literally. 'I haven't had a wink of sleep since herself started movin' up there above,' one woman told me. 'The roads are jammed with cars and buses, not to mention people and the streets are noisy until all hours in the morning.' Another local lad was quite categorical . . . it's a fuckin' bollix, like. You can't fuckin, get home, I swear – I fuckin' have to walk, fuck it. . .
>
> Some claim a hoax: 'Well, I'll tell ye, if you look . . . you'll see a wire running down the hill. . . I'm getting a percentage.'
>
> . . . One holy father who wouldn't give his name stumbled into me by mistake, but he was willing to give an opinion:
>
> 'Technically, I'm ferry pleezed at the numbers dere like. . . De atmosphere is ferry wholesome. It's bringing ush back to a religish strength in dis country which de media are trying to pash off as superstitioshion. . .'

The 'moving' statue at Ballinspittle and later reports of other similar phenomena right across Ireland received their quota of radio and television reporting too. Among those to visit was BBC2 reporter Paul Barry and camera crew. Their report was one of the more professional seen by this writer. This is how it was introduced to the British audience:

> . . . Early this year four girls believe they saw a vision of the Virgin Mary in the night sky in Sligo. This is just one of the latest of more than thirty reports of apparitions and moving statues at religious shrines across Ireland during the last eight weeks. To a secular English audience it may seem hard to take such things seriously, to many in Ireland

> it is emphatically not a joke. Whether it's mass hysteria or a sign from heaven, believer and non-believer alike have no doubt that something very unusual is happening there. . .

During the fifteen minute report an accurate and objective account of events to date was given including interviews with members of the local committee. During the programme Pat Bowen, secretary of the committee instanced three separate 'miracles' which they believed had occurred at the shrine.

One point highlighted was the determination of the committee not to allow the area to be commercialised. Councillor Denis O'Reilly spoke: 'We're not going to commercialise this under any circumstances, that is definite. While I'm there and while there's any life in my body or blood in my veins I will not allow this to be commercialised. We want to keep it as a holy place, a place for devotion and we intend doing that. There is great devotion here and we believe that this is supernatural.'

The reporter Paul Barry saw the statue 'move' himself, 'though to be sure, when you stare at a small pool of light, the eye can play tricks.'

Later the report took the most peculiar twist of all. While filming at Mount Melleray – where Our Lady is reputed to have appeared to some children – the BBC lighting crewman saw the vision: 'The whole hill around the statue just went into one single mass of greenery. 'Twas a cloud come to surround the statue and Our Lady's face turned into Our Lord's. Her veil turned into long hair. I just shook my head to bring myself back to reality and she came back clear for a second but instantly then it changed back into Our Lord again. It's frightening, I couldn't believe it.' And the final word to Bishop Murphy. He told the crew: 'Maybe you might have an epidemic in England!'

And indeed, according to Paul Barry, miracles and visions were common in England some 500 years ago. As to why they should come to Ireland in such numbers in the twentieth century 'it says much about the people, and more about the country. It could have happened almost nowhere else.'

In Ireland for many a news item has not been fully aired unless discussed on the *Late Late Show*. On Friday, 13 September, the opening night of the autumn season Gay Byrne produced for eager viewers a recorded on-the-spot report from Culleens, Co. Sligo where four local schoolgirls believe they saw a vision of Our Lady on Monday, 2 September. However, the show was dominated by the appearance of two lesbian ex-nuns whose presence had been widely publicised during the preceding week.

The leader of Ireland's Democratic Socialist Party, Alderman Jim Kemmy, a Limerick stone mason issued a statement on the 'moving' statue on 19 September. He described the phenomenon as 'a turning away from reality.' Alderman Kemmy said that moving statues had become a feature of Limerick life as elsewhere. 'Prospects are so bleak, unemployment is so bad and it has been such a terrible year weatherwise, that we are all suffering from third world hallucinations. There is even talk that the end of the world is near,' he said. He added that as a public representative he wanted to dispel such notions. 'We should turn towards life, towards our young people and find some answers ourselves to our problems. At the moment we are opting out of life,' he said. Alderman Kemmy pointed out that he had been a stone mason for more than thirty years and is very familiar with the materials that most of those statues are made from. There is, he said, no chemical process by which the statues could move. 'Cracks from wear and tear and expansion from stone in water is common but there is no other movement. They have no powers of animation.'

He remarked that people who said that they had seen things were experiencing optical illusions or suffering from mass hysteria. Hallucinations like this, he said, are common in third world countries where conditions are so bleak 'but there is no comfort in moving statues.'

On Friday night, 20 September former TD and Minister,

Dr Conor Cruise O'Brien who is also a professed agnostic visited Ballinspittle at the invitation of David Hanly of the RTE News Features Department. A report on the visit was given on the *This Week* programme on Sunday, 22 September. In Kinsale town Dr O'Brien gave his opinion before arriving at the grotto:

> I don't expect to have my curiosity satisfied tonight. I am not totally open-minded. I think it is extremely improbable that such phenomena have been genuinely witnessed. I think it very probable people think they have seen something of the kind.
>
> I think it very likely that there may have been quite natural phenomena like those produced by staring continuously at some object which would produce strange sense impressions. I don't expect to find anything that will lead me to believe that there is a supernatural phenomenon here and even if I did see something that I thought was a movement I would be very sceptical about the sense impressions that I had thought myself to have received. But I would certainly be interested in that.

For two minutes Dr O'Brien stared up at the lighted statue. Did he see anything? 'No,' replied Dr O'Brien, 'as far as I can see it is a perfectly genuine statue and as motionless as you would expect it to be.' However, he did have some remarkable observations to make. It surprised him 'how much it is a middle-class manifestation.' He was not impressed by any faith he witnessed at the shrine. 'I don't find anything intrinsically moving about people who come expecting to see a statue move or behave in other improbable ways and then become convinced that they have seen it. I find that on the whole rather disquieting and a bit depressing and not impressive in a favourable way.'

Dr O'Brien continued:

> Also it seemed to me for some of those we talked to at least, that it wasn't really a religious experience. It didn't

> seem to be anything that was going to change their lives significantly. It was just a wonder, a strange thing worth coming out to see or to think that you saw. . . I think it rather disturbing that if people are that credulous or that bored, and a sizeable number of the middle-class, I don't think that is auspicious for the future either of the economy or of the polity. If, for example, a lot of voters are that credulous they could rather easily move over to some other charismatic leader whom they believed to be 'moving' in the right way.

Dr O'Brien of course discreetly refrained from naming who such a leader might be! So also do the writers of this book.

3: More Than One Moving Statue

The following is a brief look at reported apparitions and 'moving' statues in Ireland. The list is of necessity incomplete as some reports were not very widely publicised. Included, however, are the main locations reported, prior to and during 1985. Significantly the highest concentration is in the Limerick/Kerry area followed by west Leinster and south Munster. To date there have been no reported sightings of 'moving' statues in Northern Ireland.

Prior to 1985:

A. **Knock.** On the evening of 2 August, 1879 in the village of Knock, Co. Mayo an apparition of Our Lady, St Joseph and St John the Evangelist was seen on the gable-end of the local church. In all there were fifteen eye-witnesses. The apparition at Knock is the only one in Ireland recognised by the Church and along with Lourdes and Fatima is counted among the chief Marian shrines in the world. However the Vatican has never officially confirmed that an apparition took place nor is belief in any of the three location a requirement of the Catholic faith. The investigation into Knock was not set up until 1936 by Bishop T. P. Gilmartin and lasted three years, some sixty years after the first reported apparition.

B. **Templemore.** On 15 August 1920 a number of bleeding statues were reported in a house in the town of Templemore, in north Tipperary. Thousands flocked to the house and upwards of fifty sets of crutches were reportedly abandoned.

C. **Kerrytown.** On 11 January 1939 an apparition of the Virgin Mary was reported in the north Donegal village of Kerrytown. It was first reported by Teresa Ward and other

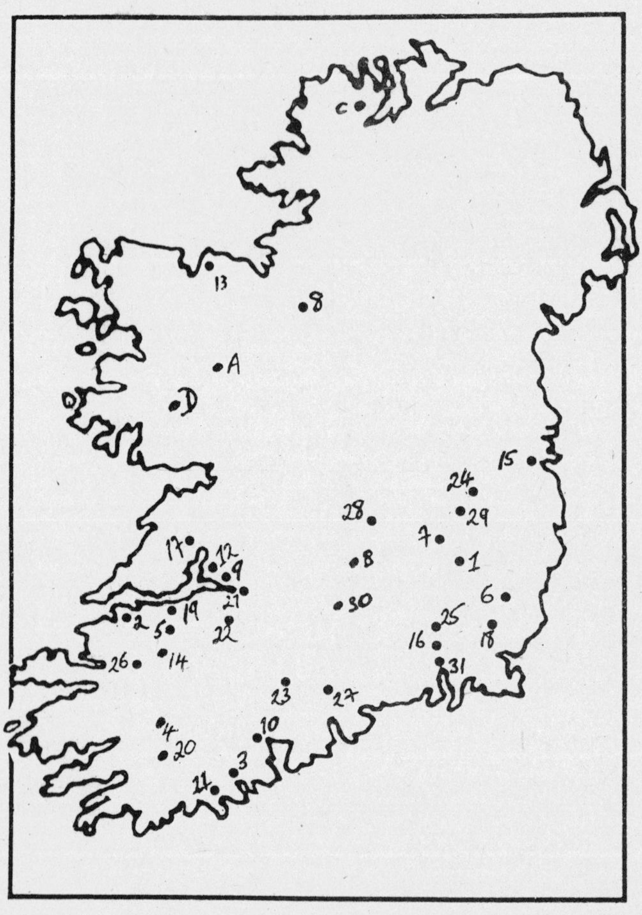

A. Knock
B. Templemore
C. Kerrytown
D. Cornamona

1. Abbeyleix
2. Asdee
3. Ballinspittle
4. Ballydesmond
5. Cahermoyle
6. Camolin
7. Carlow
8. Carrick-on-Shannon
9. Coollard
10. Cork
11. Courtmacsherry
12. Cratloe
13. Culleens
14. Currow
15. Dublin
16. Dunkitt
17. Glenbrien
18. Enniscorthy
19. Foynes
20. Inchigeelagh
21. Limerick
22. Mainster
23. Mitchelstown
24. Monasterevin
25. Mooncoin
26. Mountcollins
27. Mount Melleray
28. Roscrea
29. Stradbally
30. Tipperary
31. Waterford

members of her family. They claimed to have seen the apparition on a large slab of granite in a field next to their house. The village became a centre of pilgimage from 1939 to 1946.

D. **Cornamona.** On 10 May 1947 an apparition of Our Lady was reported in the town of Cornamona in Co. Galway. The vision was first seen by Mary Moran, a local girl.

1985

Asdee. On 14 February the first report in 1985 of a 'moving' statue came from Asdee in Co. Kerry. There a group of children claimed to have seen a statue of Our Lady and child, at the back of the church, open its eyes and move its hands. Other witnesses followed up with similar claims. The church became a place of pilgrimage for some months but numbers have now diminished.

Abbeyleix. A number of people claimed to have seen a statue move in the grounds of the local church.

Ballinspittle. Almost half a million people have now visited the shrine in Ballinspittle, in south-west Cork where seven local people claim to have seen the statue of Our Lady move on 22 July. Some seventy per cent of all pilgrims claim to see some movement and many have also said they witnessed the transformation of the face to that of Our Lord. The grotto in Ballinspittle is Ireland's best known 'moving' statue and reports there led to a multiplication of parallel claims up and down the country.

Ballydesmond. In Ballydesmond, Co. Cork a group of children claimed to have seen a statue outside the town move. Their parents later dismissed the idea.

Cahermoyle. In Cahermoyle, Co. Limerick a local man claimed to have seen a statue of Our Lady in the area move.

Camolin. Following reports of a moving statue in Camolin, Co. Wexford local people gathered to say the rosary and sing hymns.

Carlow. A small glass-covered image on Rossmore Hill some three miles outside the town is reported to have moved. The statue was originally located in a coal mine.

Carrick-on-Shannon. A young local girl claimed to have seen the statue of Our Lady in the grounds of the local convent move.

Coolard. In Coolard, Co. Limerick sixteen local children say they saw the statue of the Virgin Mary at the local shrine move. Many came to pray there following the report.

Cork City. There have been at least two reports of moving statues in Cork city, one at the shrine in Curragheen and the other in the Church of the Resurrection, Farranree.

Courtmacsherry. A local Protestant youth and his girlfriend were the first to report movement in the statue at Courtmacsherry, Co. Cork. A priest also said he saw the statue 'swaying back and forth' for more than an hour.

Cratloe. People gathered to pray at the shrine in Cratloe in Co. Limerick after two women from a local prayer group said they saw it move. Others claimed to have seen the face of Christ and Padre Pio on the statue.

Culleens. Thousands gathered at Carns, Culleens, Co. Sligo after four local girls reported seeing an apparition of Our Lady. Many claimed to see various visions in the night sky overhead.

Currow. A number of adults claimed to have seen tears in the eyes and the hands move in the statue of the Sacred Heart in Kilteentierna church, Currow, Co. Kerry. Others said they saw movement in the statue of the Blessed Virgin.

Dublin. There have been some reports of a moving statue in the grounds of the Oblate Church in Inchicore though these have been dismissed by the priests. There have been very few reports of 'moving' statues in Dublin or other large urban centres.

Dunkitt. Many local people at Dunkitt, Co. Waterford claimed to have seen a statue in the local shrine move on several occasions.

Glenbrien. In Glenbrien, Co. Clare two women claimed they saw a local statue move. Since then many gathered to sing and pray.

Enniscorthy. A number of women in Enniscorthy, Co. Wexford claimed to see a statue move as they left the House of Missions building.

Foynes. A local woman in Foynes, Co. Limerick claimed to have seen a statue in the grotto move.

Inchigeelagh. Two young girls twice reported seeing an apparition of the Blessed Virgin in the mid-Cork village of Inchigeelagh. Some twenty years previously another girl also claimed to have seen an apparition there. When she died at an early age the shrine, where the recent apparitions appeared, was built by the girl's father.

Limerick. People reported seeing the statue at Garryowen in Limerick city bleed and as a result many have come there to pray.

Mainster. A local man claimed to see the statue in the shrine at Mainster, Co. Limerick move.

Mitchelstown. The only recent reported appearance of the devil 'with horns' occurred in Mitchelstown, Co. Cork. Local girls also claimed that Our Lady appeared and said the word 'peace'.

Monasterevin. Several hundred people have turned up at a statue of the Blessed Virgin close to St Evin's Park, Monasterevin, Co. Kildare since a local woman claimed to have seen the white three foot statue open its right eye and close it again. Others claim to have seen blood coming from the right eye.

Mooncoin. A group of young men claimed they saw the statue in the local shrine move. One girl claimed to have seen a tear fall from the right eye and that the left eye opened and closed.

Mountcollins. One of the reports to come soon after Ballinspittle was that of a moving statue in Mountcollins, Co. Limerick. Some claimed to have seen manifestations of the Sacred Heart.

Mount Melleray. There a teenage girl and two boys claimed to have seen an apparition of Our Lady who also spoke and gave a warning of a great disaster in the next decade unless people turned back to prayer.

Roscrea. Locals claimed they saw the statue of the Virgin Mary in the grounds of St Anne's Convent, Roscrea, Co. Tipperary move. The nuns denied the claim.

Stradbally. In Stradbally, Co. Laois locals claimed they saw the statue of the Blessed Virgin bleed and transform into the face of Christ.

Tipperary. Girls in the Convent of Mercy primary school in Tipperary town claimed to have seen the statue of Katherine McCauley, who founded the order, move. One local nun recommended that 'they visit the church and say their prayers'.

Waterford. Two young boys claimed to have seen the statue outside the Mercy convent move and that Our Lady spoke of Pope John Paul II being assassinated.

4: The Psychologists move in

Science is forever trying to put things into neat little boxes. If something won't go in, then science usually ignores it. At first the 'Ballinspittle effect', as I began to call it, went quite neatly inside a little box in my mind labelled 'visual effects'. Of course, it took a bit of puzzling out, but I was sure, and the rest of my team was also sure, that we had it sorted out. As the weeks went by, it became clear to me that there was a lot happening that could not be included in 'visual effects'. I now have several other little boxes in my mind but it is also fair to say that some of the things we have discovered just won't go into any of them.

Now, what would you do if you were a scientist?

On the one hand, I just can't ignore things. If strange events happen, then it is my job, and the job of every other scientist, to try to find out why. If nobody ever wondered 'why?', we'd still be sitting in caves, afraid of the lightning. On the other hand, many of the things that have happened have been private to individuals. As psychologists, my team and I have to respect this privacy and the good faith of the people who have experienced these things. These are parts of the ethics of our profession.

So if something strange happens, I can't ignore it, and I must fit it into the pattern of science. If concrete statues begin to move today, where do we go from there? Will I be able to trust the back axle of my car?

It became clear to us that there were two aspects to the Marian apparitions of the summer. One was a public aspect. Some things were experienced and witnessed by many thousands of people, including ourselves. We can give fairly strong and confident scientific explanations of these because we can do experiments on ourselves. The other aspect is the private one. All we can do here is offer much more tentative explanations based on our knowledge of psychology and sociology.

Of course, many people aren't bothered by the strange and the unexpected. To them it's just the way things are, and they're quite happy to leave things they can't explain as a mystery. In fact, I talked to a journalist in Dublin about the 'Ballinspittle effect' who said, 'You're a terrible lot of spoilsports. Why can't you let people have their fun?'

Well, here are the theories. If you think there are things which will always be beyond our understanding, that's up to you. On the other hand, if what you've seen and heard seriously disturbs you, and you want to see if there is a possibility of a scientific explanation, then read on. . .

But I don't guarantee that I can explain everything.

Towards the end of July, Donna O'Sullivan, a well-known presenter with the RTÉ Cork Local Radio telephoned me. 'Have you been down to Ballinspittle, Jurek?' she asked. 'Can you give us the point of view of the psychologist?' I'd just come back from a heavy scientific meeting in Brussels but I agreed to come and talk the following day. That afternoon, I drove down to Ballinspittle and saw the shrine in daylight. There seemed to be nothing terribly strange about it. I examined it from the roadside and from the hill opposite. I looked at it with binoculars and with the naked eye. It looked like one of many hundreds of wayside shrines that I had become familiar with since my arrival in Ireland.

Since I couldn't come down at night, I talked to people at the shrine and later, when I returned to Cork, to other people around the city. Most of the people in Cork I talked to had already been or were soon going. I asked those who were going that night to make a special note of what they saw and told them that I'd look them up the following day, if they had no objection, to talk about what they'd experienced.

Talking to people in this way is not easy. You can't ask them leading questions like 'What way did it move?' and scientific honesty does not let you 'take sides' for or against. I simply told whoever I spoke to that I was a psychologist from the college, that I was interested in the happenings at Ballinspittle, and had they seen anything when they were there. I began to collect a mass of data of which I tried to make some sense. Eventually, I had spoken to about sixty people who had been at Ballinspittle. The reports my team and I collected seemed to agree with reports that we heard on the radio and read in the newspapers. The salient facts seemed to be as follows:

1. If anything happened, it happened in the twilight or early evening.
2. About 80% of the people I talked to had seen some sort of movement.
3. The movements seen were movements of the whole of the lighted portion of the statue: they could have been left-right movements, front-back, 'jittering' up and down movements, slow, swaying movements. A well-spoken and elegant lady I spoke to gave me a clue that for the moment I couldn't put into place: she said she observed that the rosary which hung from the statue's hands seemed to move *with the statue*. It did not move independently of the statue, as it would if a live person were swaying holding a rosary from their hands. I was to remember that remark of hers later.
4. A lot of people who had seen the movements were profoundly disturbed by what they had seen. They asked me if they had been hallucinating or if they had been in the grip of some sort of hysteria. Many were convinced there was a rational explanation for what they had seen and they asked me if I had any opinions on the matter. I told them that at the moment, I had no idea, but that if I developed a theory, I'd pass it on to them for what it was worth.
5. Everybody agreed that the atmosphere at the shrine was calm, and even peaceful. 'It was very restful,' one lady told me. 'Even though I'd been on my feet all day I just stayed there and watched and prayed. I could have stayed there for hours, but my husband wanted to get back home.' Her husband is a professional lorry driver and has to get up at

unheard-of hours. It also struck me as significant that he hadn't seen anything moving. 'But there was definitely no hysteria there,' he said.

I kept these five facts in my mind when I faced Donna's penetrating questions the following lunchtime. But I refused to be drawn into denying a miracle. I could see Donna was nettled, and that she had perhaps been hoping that I was going to play the sceptic. If I was cautious, I was in good company. A recorded interview with the Bishop of Cork showed that he was also keeping an open mind about the whole thing.

That evening I had arranged to go to Ballinspittle to see the shrine. I called in, as arranged, to the flat where one of my postgraduate students lived. This was Lenny Stapleton. He is doing his Masters on the visual effects of movement, and under my guidance, he had read and met many of the psychologists who were considered experts in this field. I trusted his judgement and knew of the scrupulous accuracy with which he carried out his experiments. At his flat, an old friend of ours had dropped in quite by chance. This was to be the third member of our team: Jim Good. Jim is a computer specialist, at present working in industry, but he had worked in our department and it was always a pleasure to hear him dissect a problem with his keen, analytical brain.

We set off for Ballinspittle in subdued spirits. We were facing a big unknown, and had no notion of how it might turn out. We began to encounter the Ballinspittle traffic just after Cork airport, but it didn't slow us down too much until after Kinsale.

We left the car where the steward directed us and walked for twenty minutes or so to the shrine. The local committee had erected a barrier across the road at the shrine, and we came up to them and explained who we were. I spoke to an elderly gentleman and offered to show him my ID from the college, but he told me he believed me. There was some doubt as to whether we should first of all go down to meet other members of the shrine committee, but in the end he decided that it wouldn't be necessary. He detailed a young local lad to keep us company and to answer our questions.

The only reason I'm going into this detail about what happened is because later on, allegations were made that we hadn't been there at all! If Christian charity and honesty rules the day, at least those two people we talked to should have pointed out that they had seen and talked to us that evening. Perhaps they did, but that sort of thing doesn't make as much news as misinformed comments about 'bespectacled atheists from the college'.

I saw the statue moving.

Jim did too. Lenny didn't.

We saw it moving from the road, and from the kneelers at the table of flowers at the foot of the slope.

We saw it moving when we looked up with our naked eyes and when we used the high-powered binoculars I had brought along. Even Lenny saw it moving with the binoculars.

I walked around, gazing up at the statue, and joined in with the prayers. I was aware of the atmosphere: it was peaceful and there was a genuine feeling of devotion. People were praying, or just standing and watching. Some were following the prayers with their rosaries. We did not disturb anybody there, and we talked to each other in hushed tones.

I knew that when I used binoculars that my hands were none too steady, and so I tried to rest the binoculars on a wooden pole which was holding a wire fence up. The statue seemed to stop moving until Jim accidentally pushed against the wire. Very soon we were all able to make the statue appear to move or not while looking through the binoculars resting on the post, just by strumming the wire of the fence with our fingers.

'OK,' I said. 'We've sorted out why it might appear to move for people with binoculars. Let's get up close and see if we can see why it appears to move for people without them.' Kneeling close, on the road by the table with the flowers, we looked up. The statue seemed to have stopped moving for me.

Lenny whispered into my ear, 'Try moving your head to and fro very quickly.' I did, while looking at the statue, and

I saw the same movement I had seen earlier. Lenny held Jim's head gently from behind at the level of the ears, and shook it very lightly. All I heard from Jim was a soft 'Wow.'

Once we'd all tried the head movements on our own and with help we moved back and had a quiet discussion. It was Jim with his local knowledge of the area, who suggested that we go down to Belgooly, on the other side of Kinsale, and try our observations out on a similar statue there.

We thanked the young man who'd been showing us around. 'Do you think you know why it's moving?' he asked.

'It's something to do with head movements,' I told him, 'but we're not sure yet. We're going to have to do some hard thinking.' We thanked the people at the barrier, and said we'd let them know if we came up with anything sensible. I remember that going back to the car, we got involved in a serious discussion.

There is a phenomenon well-known in psychology called the 'wandering light' or 'autokinetic' effect. This takes place in a totally darkened room. You attach a small point source of light to one of the walls and just look at it. After a minute or so, that little point source of light appears to move. It will move left, right, sweep around in half circles. You begin to wonder whether it hasn't got loose from where you stuck it on to the wall, but no, when you turn on the light to check it's exactly where you left it before. The explanation is that in the total darkness, your visual sense begins to lose track of where you are, or where your eyes are in relation to the rest of you. I was reluctant to try and extend that explanation to what we had seen because even at night, there was enough light around us for us to see where we were going. Jim was able to read his watch. The autokinetic effect doesn't work if there is *any* light around. On the other hand, I remembered that pilots at night are advised to line up points of light against features on the inside of their cockpit if they need to check if those lights are moving or stationary.

Our discussion turned to the theories of James Gibson, and I remembered work I had done on the visul control of movement in the laboratory of my old mentor, David Lee, back in Edinburgh.

'Jimmy' Gibson was an American psychologist who had been dissatisfied with the traditional accounts of visual perception which had held sway in psychology from the 1890s. His favourite 'fall guy' had been the great German physiologist and psychologist, Helman von Helmholtz. Von Helmholtz had done many experiments on visual perception in his laboratories, but to Gibson, these experiments had been done in a highly contrived setting, putting observers in total darkness and making them look at small points and discs of light.

When Jimmy had joined the Second World War effort as a psychologist, giving training to soldiers and airmen in visual perception, he realised that you had to take into account the totality of the perceptual situation: when a soldier was trying to estimate the speed and distance of a moving object, he was relating that object to the ground and other features of the visual environment he saw. After the war, Jimmy Gibson elaborated his theory in a series of books that by now have become classics in the field of visual research. *Ecological Optics* was his last and remains the clearest and most succinct statement of his theory. He was concerned to do research in normal visual conditions, in outdoor settings, in the full light of day. His research was like a breath of fresh air in the rather stuffy confines of traditional theories of visual perception. He called his theory 'Ecological Optics' because he was concerned with the relationship of the visual process and the setting in which it had evolved, the normal visual environment.

David Lee studied with Jimmy at Cornell, and while I was working with Dave, Jimmy came over several times for exciting seminars and discussions with his former student and *his* students. Dave Lee had elaborated a theory of Jimmy's which stated basically that it is our eyes which give us the most precise information about our position relative to the rest of our environment. For instance, if you shut your eyes, you sway more than if your eyes are open. Your eyes give you direct feedback about your body position. Your mind seems to prefer the information from your eyes to the information from your body joints and muscles, and from the so-called 'semi-circular canals' in the vestibular system of your ears.

One of the most striking demonstrations of the importance of the visual sense in maintaining posture was the series of experiments we called the 'swinging room experiments'. The swinging room was a cubicle consisting of three walls and a ceiling, large enough to walk around in, which was suspended from the real ceiling of the laboratory with about two inches clearance off the laboratory floor. We were able to attach this structure to a small electric motor, and we were able to electronically record (a) the movement of the room, and (b) the movement of a person standing in the room. What we found was that when we started the room gently swinging to and fro (about 2 cms in either direction) a person standing inside, looking at the walls, was not aware of the room moving. When we looked at the movement of the person inside that room we found that he or she would be swaying with the room to keep the visual distance between themselves and the walls constant. The amazing thing was, the person was quite unaware of their movement! The information from their visual sense over-rode the information from their joints and their vestibular system.

Dave Lee's students were always experimenting with the swinging room set-up, on themselves and on people who hadn't heard about it. The effect never seemed to wear off with practice, and we never found anybody who was able to resist the gentle movement of the swinging room. One particular incident remained in my mind. A celebrated psychologist had heard about Dave's set-up, and came to Edinburgh specially to see for himself. We got everything going as normal, and we were getting nice even traces on our equipment of the man's movements in time with the movements of the room, when we heard his voice booming from inside the swinging room: 'Well, David, when is your experiment starting?'

Travel sickness is to a large extent generated by the fact that your body tells you you *are* moving (the swaying of a ship in high seas or the violent accelerations and decelerations of a car

The scene at the Grotto in Mount Melleray, Co. Waterford on 27 August 1985.

The statue of Our Lady at Courtmacsherry, Co. Cork.

The statue at Ballinspittle.

Photograph taken by Eddie O'Hare on 24 July

Pilgrims gazing at the statue of Our Lady in Ballinspittle

(photo : Eddie O'Hare)

do register with your vestibular system) but your visual sense tells you that you aren't, perhaps because you're inside a ship's cabin or because you're staring down at your lap, afraid to look out of the window. The conflict between your senses causes nausea. Our message to people who get sick is to look out of the window at something fixed: like the horizon. The sensations from your body and from your visual sense will then be in harmony and the nausea should ease off.

Coming back to the events at Ballinspittle, we eventually came to the conclusion that in the darkness of twilight or night, people just don't have enough visual information to tell them about the natural movement of their body. We do not usually spend our time standing in fields at night looking at a small lighted statue several hundred yards away. If your body starts to sway or the muscles in your neck start to tremble, the image in your eye of the statue will move. If you have no idea you are moving, you are likely to attribute the movement to the lighted portion of the statue rather than to yourself. People who have a lot of experience of the finer points of visual perception (for instance, lorry drivers or cameramen) are more resistant to the effect. Since it is yourself that's really moving, you will tend to see the entire lighted portion of the statue moving as a solid mass, rosary and all.

(A point that only emerged later, when television crews began to converge on Ballinspittle, was that when the entire shrine was flooded with strong light, the statue appeared to cease moving for most people. The effect of the strong light would be to connect the statue visually with a lot more of the immediate environment. From our discussion above, it would follow that the statue should cease to seem to move.)

We repeated our observations at the Belgooly shrine, and got the same sorts of results, even though this shrine has no record of moving. In fact, a number of people had drawn up their cars at the car park opposite the shrine, taking a rest from the incessant traffic we now found going back to Cork – or perhaps just checking out their own theories about why statues seemed to move?

Our antics obviously attracted attention, and we explained who we were and what our theory was to this group of strangers. One man *demanded* to see my ID, although how much of it he was able to read in the darkness I don't know. Result: several people who hadn't been able to see any movement at Ballinspittle now said they could see the Belgooly statue moving. Some people who has seen the statue at Ballinspittle move said that now the Belgooly statue seemed to move in the same way as what they had seen at Ballinspittle. One man was not convinced at all, one lady said that although the halo on the Belgooly statue seemed to move when she did what we suggested, the rest of the statue didn't. We got better than an eighty per cent success rate, all told. By this stage, we were fairly sure that our explanation was holding water, but there were two additional points that didn't fit in.

The first was that when you looked at the statue and shook your head, the surrounding grotto did not seem to move. The second was: if the effect depends on you not knowing that you're moving, how come you get the effect when somebody shakes your head for you?

The discussion of these remaining two points took us most of the way back to Cork.

The eye is a truly amazing structure. I personally think that it's one of the most convincing proofs of God's existence that such a marvellous structure exists. Our discussion focused on that part of the eye called the retina. This is a light-sensitive portion of the eye, on the inside of the eyeball, directly opposite the eye lens. The function of the retina is to register light information and then to pass it on to the brain.

It is now well-known that the retina is composed of two fairly distinct areas. One, right in the middle, like the bull's eye of a dartboard, is called the fovea. This is an extremely sensitive portion of the retina, and when we are doing something intricate, we quite spontaneously turn our eyes so that what we are looking at falls exactly on the fovea. The size this area projects on our visual world is quite small. If you hold your arm out straight in front of you, raise your thumb, and look at your thumbnail, that is the size of the projection of your foveal area. The fovea is good for detail and colour vision.

Surrounding the foveal area is what is known as the periphery. The further you get away from the fovea, the less colour vision you get, and the less the acuity of the eye. The neuropsychologist Colwyn Trevarthen has spoken of the two areas as separate sub-systems in vision.

Now normally, our eyes work in a well-co-ordinated manner. For instance, the brain 'fills in' a lot of the missing information in the peripheral area; we are quick to move our eyes to the source of movement in the periphery; we as a rule don't notice that we have these two sub-systems in the retina. And yet, in exceptional visual circumstances, such as when we look at a small lighted grotto on a distant hillside, the close co-ordination between the sub-systems of the retina breaks down. The sensitive portion of the fovea registers movement of the statue; the less sensitive peripheral area does not register movement of the surround. If you look at the lighted *side* of the grotto and shake your head, the surround will appear to move, but the statue will appear to stay still!

The second problem was why do we get the moving effect when our heads are being gently shaken for us by someone else. Now the head is quite a heavy piece of the body, and once it is set in movement, it has a fair amount of inertia.

Let us take the example of someone nodding their head up and down. The muscles of the head and neck start the head in its downward track until it is moving quite fast. After a fraction of a second, we have to stop this downward movement, and initiate the reverse, upward movement. Another set of muscles comes into play, to bring the head back up again. But this second set of muscles has also to overcome the head's inertia. That is, they are straining up, and the brain thinks they are moving the head up, but the head is still either moving down, or stationary. Result: a mis-match (for a very brief while) between what the head is doing and what the brain thinks the head is doing. Now normally, in a well-lit environment, we are aware of what is happening because our visual sense is able to locate the position of the head in relation to the rest of the visual world. Again, in the Ballinspittle effect, we just don't have all that information and the statue will appear to move in the direction opposite to the one in which our head is beginning to move. If someone else is shaking our head for us, this inertia effect is a lot stronger, especially if we have relaxed our neck muscles ever so much.

By the time we had reached the Wilton roundabout, we had the essence of our explanation thrashed out. However, I still had the feeling that there were a lot of things that we had not managed to fit into our nice, neat box labelled 'visual effects'.

5: All in the Head – Or is It?

The previous evening's activities had sorted out a lot of things for us, and the following day we tried to put the rest of what we knew about the Ballinspittle phenomenon into the picture we were building up. None of us had ever met anybody who was claiming to have seen a transformation of the statue, but we were aware that a number of witnesses did claim to have seen this happen. I read a number of newspaper reports through carefully. A number of things seemed to be happening:

1. The face of the statue might be seen to smile; its eyes might turn into a particular colour; the face might take on an expression of sorrow.
2. Another face might be seen to be superimposed on the statue's face. Most commonly reported were faces 'of Christ', and Padre Pio.
3. Later, we heard that some people had seen the statue move its arms, or seen the cloak 'billowing' in the breeze.

In many ways, these reports were easier to explain from the point of view of psychology. On the other hand, because they were essentially private matters, we could not treat them in the same experimental way we had with the phenomenon of the total movement.

However, as I was bringing my facts together, I got a vivid flashback to one of my earliest experiences in a psychological laboratory. At Edinburgh, the professor of the department in my day was a small Cornish man called David Vowles who was a world authority on neuropsychology, but who also, rather unusually for a man of his eminence, took the start of the undergraduate experimental laboratory course.

In the opening classes, we had to look at a number of illusions and visual effects and report as accurately as possible on what we had seen. This was excellent training in observation and reportage. Professor Vowles' handling of the discussion sessions after the tests was inspiring. He insisted that we explain to the rest of the class exactly what *we* had seen, not what we thought we should have seen or what we might have liked to have seen. 'What you have experienced is your own personal reaction,' he would say. 'Nobody can tell you that you are wrong or that what you saw was impossible. What you have been seeing is real to you and nobody can take that away from you.' Many a student began only then to understand the complexity of the workings of the visual system and the mind, and the tremendous scope there is in this world for differences between individuals.

So I stress again, that what the witnesses at Ballinspittle and other shrines have seen *is* real for them: it is a valuable personal experience. For many, these have been valuable religious experiences. In what follows, I will try to give an explanation of how these important experiences might have come about.

It has long been known in psychology that what we see is not determined by the light entering the eye alone. In a very real sense, 'there is more to sight than meets the eye'. In particular our past experiences and our expectations play an important role in influencing what we are going to see. A lot of the research was done with ambiguous pictures or with images that were presented in difficult visual conditions. But one very elegant experiment demonstrated that even under very good visual conditions people can easily misperceive what their eyes are telling them. Mike Heffernan is a recent graduate from University College, Cork, and he worked with me on just this sort of problem.

His experiment was quite simple. He showed people a photograph which was very easily identified as an unfurled golf umbrella lying on some grass, with a man just behind and to one side of it. This photograph was called our 'target' photograph. He showed it at the end of one of two sequences of photographs. In one sequence, many of the photographs had to do with hang gliders: this was the 'hang glider' sequence. In the other sequence, the photographs were about a lot of different thing with no reference to hang gliders or umbrellas. This was what we called the 'no context' sequence.

People were given one of the sequences, and were told to look at each photograph and to identify what they saw as quickly as possible without rushing, and then to pass on to the next one in the sequence. At the end of each sequence, they were all shown the target photograph. He found that when people looked at the photographs at the end of the no context sequence, the target photograph was identified correctly 13 times out of 15. At the end of the hang glider sequence, however, the target photograph was correctly identified only 6 times out of 15. In other words, 9 times out of 15, people mis-identified the target photograph at the end of the hang glider sequence, even though the visual conditions were very good, and the photograph itself was quite unambiguous. In a subsidiary experiment, when the same target photograph was shown under only very slightly hazy visual conditions, the error rate shot up to a full 100%. A simple but elegant statistical treatment of the results showed that the probability of getting such results purely by chance was less than two times out of a hundred. This constitutes very strong proof of Mike's experiment. Mike concludes his thesis by saying that many accidents at work and on the road may occur due to effects such as these acting to distort perception.

It is well known that when you gaze at a single object for more than a minute, your eyes get tired and the object begins to look hazy. You begin not to see the fine details and the general outline can also get distorted. If we add the effects of night and tiredness after a long day's work, it becomes clear that many people, staring at the lighted statue for minutes at a time, would begin to interpret things that were not actually there in the first place. What you see would be dictated more by what you expect.

Back in the department, Lenny, Jim and I talked to our resident expert on cognitive processes: Dr Pete Hampson. He agreed with our findings and theories, and added some observations of his own that made a lot of sense to us. For instance, he pointed out that human beings function best during the day. People don't work their best at night. Even night shift-workers, used to unsocial hours, find that working at night slows them down and exposes them to a greater risk of industrial accidents. He also pointed out that driving during the twilight hours poses a lot more dangers than driving during the day or after night has properly fallen. Twilight is a bad time for accurate vision.

Pete's assessment of our findings and his added comments were extremely valuable to us. That afternoon, we released our findings to the *Cork Examiner* as the quickest way we could see of getting our views known to the concerned public.

The reactions to our press announcement were on the whole favourable. We got a few appreciative letters, and many people who met us expressed appreciation that somebody had come up with a scientific explanation for something that had been puzzling or even worrying them.

One gratifying response was from the newspapers who both in Ireland and the United Kingdom usually gave a very factual account of our findings. We were particularly concerned that what we had to say would not be reported as derogatory to the many sincere witnesses whom we had talked to and who had spoken to us in good faith. As we talked to media sources we began to stress increasingly that although we had a psychological explanation of the Ballinspittle effect, this in no way detracted from the experiences people had had, or that it was necessarily the only explanation. It was just that, as psychologists, we were able to give an account which made sense to us and which seemed to hold water under testing and the critical appreciation of our colleagues.

One thing we did point out, though, was that the Ballinspittle phenomenon was a *visual effect*. Not an illusion, or a hallucination, but just a consequence of the way our visual system works. We said at the time that we wouldn't be surprised if we didn't get reports of more moving statues under similar visual conditions.

What we didn't expect was the veritable epidemic of sightings that followed on from the Ballinspittle happenings – to date, more than thirty other shrines in Ireland have produced reports. Some of the conditions are quite similar to the conditions at Ballinspittle; others are disturbingly dissimilar. The Ballinspittle shrine itself began to produce more reports that we couldn't explain.

For instance, a number of people at Ballinspittle claimed that they saw the statue moving during broad daylight. Our explanations were completely incapable of coping with that. Others at Ballinspittle and elsewhere claimed that they heard the voice of God or Our Lady speaking to them. Children saw Our Lady appear to them and to speak to them. It was claimed that several people had been cured of ailments at the Ballinspittle shrine.

St Teresa of Avila was no stranger to visionary experiences. Many of her writings are almost psychological textbooks which explain lucidly and comprehensibly that mysterious area of human experience. She divides visions into three categories. The first are the 'exterior' manifestations: those which are perceived by the eyes. She said herself that she had never experienced these. The second are what she called 'imaginary' manifestations: in these, God speaks with 'a perfect clearness' to a person. They have also been called 'seeing or hearing with the soul' since the senses, such as vision or hearing, are not stimulated but serve as a channel through which God's message passes. The third category she called the 'intellectual' manifestations, in which senses are not at all involved. She described these as a 'vision which is not seen'.

At first the reports we heard could be easily fitted into the 'exterior' manifestations of St Teresa, and we were able to give an explanation of how they might have come about through physical means. Some of the more baffling later reports are of the type St Teresa called 'imaginary'. We can only leave these to the church to invest gate. The psychology of St Teresa is in some respects light-years ahead of our more pedestrian, experimental gropings.

The stories I began to hear about the involvement of young

children, however, gave me serious concern. The world is a very puzzling place even for adults. Most of us have forgotten how confusing it must have been when we were relatively fresh in it. Children are always trying to make sense of the world according to the knowledge they have, and in the light of the experience they have gained so far. But sometimes this experience is incomplete and children make inferences that do not correspond with reality. As they grow older, they learn more about the way the world works, and they learn to dismiss these inferences as 'childish'. It is the duty of adults to bring children to an understanding of their world according to their lights.

Fantasy and play are an important part of childhood. The Swiss psychologist Jean Piaget pointed out how valuable fantasy and play are for the developing child but he also showed how important it is that these play activities should relate to the everyday world. Many younger children will have imaginary pets or friends. A youngster may have an imaginary monster friend whom he feeds bread and jam out in the back garden. Of course, mother will understand her child is acting out a fantasy, and may, if she is a caring, sensitive person, enter into the game for a while. But her child will also pick up those subtle cues from mother's behaviour that it *is* a game. A young girl may have her favourite doll whom she feeds, changes, bathes, and puts to sleep. Her doll may sometimes be tired, hungry, or want to stay up a bit more. Parents and older siblings will often join in the game, but the child soon learns the differences between dolls and people.

I became concerned that some young children might begin a fantasy play in which, perhaps, that mysterious person 'Our Lady' appeared and spoke to them. When they told their older brothers or sisters or their parents, instead of treating it as yet another instance of the fantastic creativity of the young person's mind, they were taken seriously. What started as a game suddenly begins to have disturbing follow-ons that other games never had before. The young children are taken to see many strange adults who ask difficult questions; a lot of fuss is taken about their one-time game. The children become distraught, upset and exhausted, but the extra fuss that is now made of them makes them important. They develop behaviours that normal children don't have, like staring into space for hours. Meanwhile, 'normal' development is in abeyance. . .

The vital point is that young children may not be dealing with the same sorts of concepts as adults. If an adult says 'Our Lady appeared to me and told me certain things' we can be reasonably sure (if that person is sincere) that they have had some sort of religious experience involving sight and sound. What are we to understand if a young child tells us the same thing?

A psychologist who works with young children in Glasgow, Dr Irene Neilson, showed that many young children have difficulty in understanding the difference between concepts like 'in front of', 'behind', 'on top of' and 'underneath'. Professor Margaret Donaldson is another expert in the way the minds of young children work. In her book *Children's Minds* she talks about the sorts of difficulties children have with language for everyday things. One bizarre account concerns a small experiment in which two psychologists, in talking to children, asked them the seemingly nonsense question 'is milk bigger than water?' Margaret Donaldson reports that all but one five-year-old child (who, she says, 'grinned his head off') gave solemn answers and justifications. For example: 'Because it's got a colour'.

If we have difficulty in communicating with young children about these matter-of-fact things, how much more difficult it must be to understand what they mean when they say 'Our Lady spoke to me?'

I am not saying that we should ignore what our children are telling us, or that it is impossible that God should speak to anyone under twelve. (Didn't Jesus tell us to 'suffer little children to come unto me?') But I am saying that we should be careful to consider the special conditions of childhood.

Luckily, young children are mentally very robust, even if they might be very suggestible in the short term.

There is another factor in the mental abilities of young children that may make them susceptible to all sorts of strange phenomena. This is what is called photographic, or 'eidetic' memory.

One of the best accounts of photographic memory in young children was given by the British psychologist, G. W. Allport, in 1924. Allport worked with a group of about sixty eleven-year-old children. He found that many of the children were able to conjure up a mental image of something they had seen, and were able to 'place' this image on a feature of their environment. For instance, a child might look at a picture for a few minutes. The picture could be taken away, and then the child could 'see' the picture on a nearby wall with such clarity and vividness that the picture obscured what was actually there. A striking aspect of this eidetic image is that there is a wealth of detail on it that the child might not have noticed in the first place while she was looking at the picture it came from. Allport's children were able to count buttons on coats, the number of whiskers on a cat and so on.

An American psychologist named H. Kluver was further able to get the children he was working with to induce a movement in their eidetic images. For instance, the children could make an image of a horse appear to gallop in front of their eyes. Kluver could show the children a picture of a donkey near a manger, and when the children were producing an eidetic image of the donkey, could suggest to them that the 'the donkey might be hungry', whereupon many of the children would report 'seeing' the donkey rush off to the manger and start eating.

Psychologists today have developed sophisticated tests to gauge whether someone has this photographic memory or not. A familiar test uses two pictures which when combined make up a letter of the alphabet. Looked at singly, nobody can accurately guess which letter is being represented. When a child with a photographic memory images one picture over the other, she is able to state quickly and accurately which letter it is.

Photographic memory is clearly a fascinating phenomenon.

It has been estimated that about sixty per cent of children up to the age of 12 may possess this ability. Estimates of how many adults have this ability vary: they go between one and ten per cent of the adult population. An interesting feature of photographic memory is that many children and adults are not aware that what they possess is in any way rare or special.

It is generally accepted by psychologists that photographic memory is a more rudimentary sort of memory. Because we handle so much information, our minds learn very quickly to take out the relevant details of what we see or hear and to remember just those. It is much more efficient, for instance, to remember the gist of what you have just read than to retain an image of the paragraph. However, speculations about the role of photographic memory in the various sightings reported this summer must remain just that at present – speculations. None of us has the financial resources to pursue this line of approach, and we felt that the children involved most probably had had enough people poking at them. What people see is a very private matter.

We felt that we could legitimately investigate a phenomenon such as the 'moving statue' because many thousands of people witnessed it and wanted an explanation. We felt very reluctant to invade the privacy of an individual's (especially a child's) mental life.

The final topic that began to suggest itself in our minds which could relate to the events of the summer was the fallibility of memory. This is a more speculative topic as many of the sightings were reported 'on the spot' and did not seem to involve memory in the sense of someone thinking back to events that had happened previously.

It is perhaps little appreciated that to observe what is going on and to be able to report it later without adding embellishments or distortions is a skill that takes a lot of practice. A typical experiment on eye witness testimony takes the following form.

People are shown a film clip or a series of photographs or, as in some of the original experiments, are made to witness a contrived scene that has been carefully rehearsed beforehand. Some time later, the witnesses are asked to recall as exactly as possible what happened and to write this down. The discrepancies between what people originally saw and what they reported later are alarming.

For instance, in our laboratory several years ago people were asked to watch carefully four projected slides that made up a short incident. In the first slide, two teenagers were standing on the pavement of a quiet road with a suitcase in front of them. In the second, a car is seen drawing up to them. In the third, one of the teenagers is loading the suitcase into the boot of the car, and in the fourth, the car is driving off with one teenager in the front seat next to the driver, while the other waves from the kerb.

When people were asked to write a summary of what they had seen several hours later, almost every possible discrepancy arose in the reports that could have. For instance, some people said they had definitely seen one of the teenagers thumbing the car. Some people said that both teenagers got in. Many people were unable to remember the colour of the car or asserted that the colour of the car was definitely some colour it was not.

Memory can play strange tricks on us.

Before we leave the topic of possible causes. I must mention, for sake of fairness, a theory put forward by a physicist in the College, Dr Colm O'Sullivan. He told me that it could be possible for a heat source (e.g. warmth from the day's sunlight absorbed by the rocks, heat from the bulbs themselves, or indeed some other source of heating that we haven't thought of) to increase the temperature of the cold night air around the head of the statue, thus altering the refractive index of the air in that small space. If a gentle breeze blew, it would have the effect of disturbing the mass of warmer air, and an observer would be able to see the head of the statue shimmer. He has made calculations which show that all that would be needed would be quite a small increase in the local air temperature for an effect to be seen as far away as on the hillside opposite.

While his theory could elegantly account for a movement of the head of the statue at Ballinspittle, it would not account for why we were able to 'induce' the perception of movement both at Ballinspittle and at the Belgooly shrine. He agrees with me that his theory should be put to the test before we jump to any hasty conclusions, but he sees the practical difficulties involved.

An old friend of mine, Dr Graham Manson, a medical physicist, suggested that it should be quite easy to check whether the statue is physically moving or not. There are various ways of detecting movement, using sound, light or Döppler radar. A domestic radar intruder alarm could have its aerial easily modified to provide a device suitable for detecting movement at a distance. This experiment, he pointed out, would be quite discreet and would not involve anybody climbing around the statue, as it could be done from the roadside. To date, he has not done this experiment, nor does he see the point of it. As far as he was concerned, he told me, he certainly did not believe that if God wanted to speak to us that He would do something as trivial as make a statue move a few inches in either direction every evening.

Besides which, as we both agreed, if it did happen to be a miracle, there was no telling how far the miracle would go. For instance, it could be quite possible that the miracle could extend to nullifying the ultrasonic beam, and thus, although the statue might be really moving, nothing would be recorded on the equipment!

Coming up to the feast of the Assumption, 15 August, I heard reports of people who were scared that the end of the world was about to come. A number of people since have 'heard messages' that the end of the world was about to happen on a certain date. Other reports I have received have spoken of the influence of the devil. I am sure that if we had been able to explain to these people some of the psychological mechanisms that could be involved in the reports they would have been spared needless mental anguish. The God I believe in is a just and a loving God who does not compel His people to believe in Him by fear.

I began to wonder about the social significance of all of these things happening at just this time in Ireland and why were they mostly connected with statues of Our Lady.

6: Comforter of the Afflicted

What happened at Ballinspittle sent shock waves through Irish society. Soon after, statues were seen moving and visions and manifestations of Our Lady took place at many different places which soon became places of pilgrimage. Newspapers, often stuck for a story in the 'silly season', ran stories on each new Marian manifestation as it was reported. News media in the United Kingdom and in North America began to echo the stories.

The edges of the shock wave touched the feet of the new sophisticates in Dublin. A reporter from the prestigious *Wall Street Journal* reported that the IDA in Dublin changed the topic abruptly when he brought up the subject of Ballinspittle. A technology consultant in Dublin said 'Irish of any sensitivity are obviously ashamed by this nonsense, and it is not something you should be writing about.' When the same reporter talked to the Government Information Service, the Press Secretary was unwise enough to say to the reporter 'three-quarters of the country is laughing heartily' at the antics of those folk in the south and west. The topic became a favourite butt for jokes by Mike Murphy, the presenter of a popular morning radio chat show. Many newspapers ran a lively correspondence on the topic and its implications.

Much has been made of the sightseeing aspect of this phenomenon. One explanation for the large numbers present at Ballinspittle and other shrines night after night is that this summer, the weather has been bad, and folk just have not had an excuse to get away. Religious manifestations simply offer a new sort of entertainment, and an excuse for a night out. I suspect that there is a grain of truth in this sort of account, and indeed a more old-fashioned word for this sort of excursion is 'pilgrimage'. Pilgrimages are not always serious affairs, as anybody who has read Chaucer's *Canterbury Tales* will tell

(from *Phoenix*)

Humour can be a defence reaction. . . in these contemporary cartoons we see a reaction to the multiple parallel claims.

you. However, I doubt that standing in a dark wet field for hours is anybody's idea of a substitute for the latest soap opera: the Marian apparitions are clearly offering more than just entertainment!

A friend of mine, an eminent statistical expert across the water in the United Kingdom, suggested that the rise of the apparitions could be interpreted according to a mathematical model often used in medical statistics to chart the spread of epidemics. According to this model, there is one original source (in this case the phenomena reported at Ballinspittle) and then many incidences arising from this source. In other words, a 'bandwagon effect'. In his conversation with me, he noted that the same sort of effect was seen after the Lourdes apparitions. Although his explanation makes sense statistically, it does not help us when we try to understand why the events at Ballinspittle started in the first place, or why their echoes spread over the country in the way they did.

It was clear that a lot was going on under the surface. An old explanation for the effect of humour that started with Freud is that laughter is a defence reaction which releases tension. In Cork I began to hear 'moving statue' jokes. Des MacHale, that inveterate and scholarly collector of Irish jokes, was able to tell me of at least a score that he had collected in the short space of a few weeks. Was this the emergence of a defence reaction, I asked myself. And if it was, what were people defending themselves from?

The absence of sociologists and social anthropologists surprised me. Perhaps they had had their collective fingers burnt in the 1970s when sociologists had descended in droves on little Irish villages, lived with the locals for a year, and then returned to the United Kingdom or America to write books about their analysis of what was going on between the inhabitants. This sort of activity is all well and good if you are going to study an illiterate people who won't have much chance of reading what you write; but in the case of the Irish studies, accounts of some sociologists were hurtful to the people they were writing about. The words of the investigators were often seen as being in bad taste and a breach of hospitality.

It has been a while since I read any sociology or social anthropology. In my student days my two heroes had been Bronisław Malinowski, the professor from Cracow who had spent years with the sea-going tribes of the Western Pacific, understanding their language and their myths, and Marcel Mauss who wrote the classic monograph on the social implications of gift-giving. Sociology is not an experimental science like psychology and the theories of sociologists are more speculative and have more of an intuitive feel about them than the kinds of theories with which I am habitually dealing. On the other hand, it has often been claimed that psychology, in sticking to what could be demonstrated by the experimental method, was shutting itself off from a lot of interesting phenomena simply because they could not be investigated using this method.

I began to realise that to get a fuller understanding of what was happening with regard to the Marian manifestations, I would have to cast my net wider than straight experimental psychology. My plan of research was to re-familiarise myself with some of the literature on the sociology of religion, and at the same time, to look at letters columns and talk to more people in the Cork area about what they thought.

I found that many of the letters and comments could be summarised by one of two fairly standard sociological explanations. You would most probably find a sociologist to agree with each of them. Each is probably true to some extent, but I also noticed a third strand which was independently corroborated in a startling way by a radio interview the Bishop of Cork gave to the BBC religious affairs correspondent.

Let us take a look at the two standard explanations first.

One often quoted was a version of the 'relative deprivation' hypothesis. The essence of the theory is that when things get tough economically, religious cults spring up as a sort of safety valve.

There is certainly a lot of truth in this argument. The Cork area has, in the past few years, been badly hit by unemployment. Many of the traditionally safe places of employment, such as the Ford's car assembly plant, Dunlop's tyre factory, or the Verolme dockyards had fairly recently closed down. This year's summer has been a drastic one for the farmers. The nearly incessant rain has ruined hundreds of millions of pounds worth of crops. Many small-holding farmers see ruin staring them in the face. It is said that the climatic conditions of this summer were similar to those during the terrible famine years in the nineteenth century. What sort of racial memories were being triggered?

The realities of the situation in the country were brought home to me very clearly a few weeks ago. A promising young student of ours had mentioned a few months ago that she would like to do her Master's degree research under my supervision. I met her by chance recently and happened to tell her that if she was serious, I would be interested to work with her, but she had better get her application in quickly as the deadlines were drawing close. A look of disappointment fell over her face. 'My husband is a farmer,' she told me. 'I've got to find a job to keep us over the winter.'

Even to people with a job, money does not seem to buy much. In a recent RTÉ radio programme, a number of housewives told of the struggle it was to keep their family fed and clothed. Most of the husbands of these women were in regular employment and yet they had to struggle to make ends meet. Many poor families in which the husband is working can only afford cheap cuts of meat once a week if at all. To a traditional Irish family, for which meat for dinner has become a sign of normal times and a moving away from the 'potatoes and bread' syndrome, such needs for economy have come as a serious blow to self-esteem.

Trying to cope with this level of deprivation, the argument runs, it is not surprising that people are turning to miracles.

The problem with this sort of justification is that it is also the explanation given for vandalism and hooliganism. Young people today commit crime, it is argued, because many of them are poor and unemployed, and see no hope of getting what they want any other way. As one old person sensibly commented with reference to hooligans: 'We had it tough when we were young. But we didn't go round stealing things and beating people up.'

Similarly, this explanation alone will not account for why it should be moving statues in Cork this summer. Why have people suffering deprivation in other parts of the world not been likewise visited by moving statues?

There is another angle, moreover, to the relative deprivation hypothesis which makes it distinctly dubious. If cults spring up because of deprivation, this implies that the great religions also sprang up from similar sources. I am quite cross to see Christianity, for instance, dismissed as a reaction to the way the Romans treated their slaves. If relative deprivation worked to start a religion, why can it not keep on working whenever there is a need? If bad economic conditions make people turn to religion, why didn't parish priests notice a greater attendance at mass?

The second type of reason I heard used to explain the Marian manifestations was what sociologists call the 'latent functions' argument. The essence of this theory states that if you ask why somebody follows a religion or a popular cult movement, you eventually receive answers from them which are non-rational. Not that these answers do not make sense; they are simply statements which you and they have to take on trust. Most aspects of the Christian faith, for instance, have their ultimate authority in the words of Christ. You cannot *prove* that Christ is God: taking this on faith is what makes a person a Christian. These sociologists argue that although we might give non-rational reasons for why we do something, in fact our religious practice gives us some very rational benefits which we might not even be aware of, hence the phrase 'latent functions' of religion.

What could these benefits be? Two benefits frequently cited are that (1) they serve to make sense of the world around us, and (2) they channel excitement or aggression into socially acceptable forms. Coming back to the manifestations, it is

Committee members changing the flowers at the grotto in Ballinspittle.

A young lady deep in prayer at the railings in Ballinspittle.

clear that Catholicism in Ireland is standing at the edge of the unknown. Many people feel a deep sense of anxiety and powerlessness at what they see as the growing tide of atheism and lack of regard for the traditional values of Irish society. For them, it is very timely that Our Lady should appear to her faithful and speak out against this turning-away from the church.

In the south, the traditional antipathy between Cork and Dublin manifests itself in statements about the way Dublin has grown into a soulless concrete jungle of a city. Indeed, some Dubliners I have talked to about this have spoken about the 'big cityness' of Dublin which puts the 'culchies from Cork' in their place. Dubliners see their pace of life as faster, more mechanised, and more in keeping with the tide of events in the twentieth century. They also see the south as backward, slow, mired in tradition. Southerners, by contrast, read with particular horror and lack of comprehension the tales of muggings of old people, confrontations young people have with the garda síochána, drug problems and abortion clinics with which the 'big city' seems to be rife.

Many of the comments associated with the manifestations refer explicitly to these problems that seem to be sweeping Ireland from the north-east. Thus the main 'latent function' of these manifestations is to put these problems into an explicitly religious perspective, and thus to reassure believers that God has not forsaken Ireland. All is not lost, as there is an explanation. But the message behind the manifestations also offers a cure: turn back to traditional beliefs. Many letters to newspapers stated this theme very explicitly.

Our Lady is an important figure in traditional Irish Catholicism. I know personally of many families in Ireland where the rosary and prayers for the intercession of Our Lady in their daily life are still said by the whole family at least once a week, if not daily. To those who have lost the practice of regular family prayer, the pilgrimages associated with the various places where things have happened offer an alternative outlet. At Ballinspittle in the evenings, for instance, there is a constant stream of prayers, rosaries and hymns in which the faithful gathered together join in with more enthusiasm than one ever hears at a celebration of the mass. Standing in the darkness, and looking out at a small lighted shrine gives a sense of privacy in which one can 'let go' more easily than in a well-lit church. I am always struck by the embarrassment with which many Irish church-goers meet the call to 'offer each other the sign of peace' during the communion rite, in contrast to the way this is approached in other, more exuberant cultures.

A young lady I talked to, a devout Catholic in her teens who has often been to Ballinspittle to pray at the shrine, spoke directly in these terms. 'There are things you'd do out there (i.e. the field at Ballinspittle) that you wouldn't dream of doing in a church in case people thought you were odd.'

To summarise the argument about 'latent functions'. There seem to be two main functions that the Marian manifestations serve. One is an affirmation of the Catholic way of life and a traditional Catholic interpretation (leading to downright condemnation) of the social change that is going on in Ireland; the other is an outlet for prayer and religious self-expression for people who have become self-conscious or have forgotten about the traditional ways of prayer.

A parish priest commented that instead of going around chasing statues in the countryside, his parishioners would be much better advised to join in more of the devotions at their local church. On the other hand, the message from the moving statues has reached many a conscience that may well have become relatively insensitive to the traditional message. Even the 'new sophisticates' feel defensive.

While the 'latent functions' explanation has a lot to be said for it, I am personally uncomfortable with an explanation that assumes that the sociologist is in a position of advantage over his or her fellow mortals. This manner of explanation is basically saying: 'You might think you are doing these things because of X, but I know that the real reasons for your behaviour are Y and Z, and you don't realise it.' This position might have been relatively more plausible when sociologists and social anthropologists were dealing with illiterate or semi-literate tribesmen. When we are dealing with people who are considerably more literate, educated and self-aware, the plausibility of such a position begins to fade.

Bryan Wilson, the Cambridge scholar, offers a more direct interpretation of the function of religion in his eminently readable little book called *Religion in Sociological Perspective.* All religions, he notes, try to explain the really important questions to which science cannot attain: Who are we? How did we get here? What is the 'best' way of living out our lives? What happens after we die? Religious faiths give answers to these important questions.

Implicit in his work is the idea that Christianity goes on a sort of intellectual see-saw in trying to supply the answers. From earliest times, Christianity has had a commitment to being rational and to rational argument. The works of Aristotle, for instance, were used by the early fathers of the church in order to reconcile the implications of the various myths, traditions and writings that poured forth in the first few centuries AD with the authoritative teaching of the church.

On the other hand, Christianity has also had a strong mystic, non-rational tendency. The scrolls found at Nag Hammadi and which have recently been published in translation as *The Gnostic Gospels* bear witness to this fact.

Gnosticism was outlawed as a heresy fairly early on in the history of the church. There are a number of curious beliefs connected with Gnosticism, but one that has re-appeared over and over again is the belief that God can and does speak directly to the believer, that the believer can experience direct knowledge (*gnosis* in Greek) of God without the intervention of an established church. Many of the so-called 'Gnostic Gospels' are highly personal and devotional accounts of experiences which particular believers in the first centuries AD experienced. While the church does acknowledge that some mystics do attain direct knowledge through visions and voices, St John of the Cross first stated what has since become an official line. His advice was, if you experience visions and voices, to forget them as soon as possible. Visions, he said, are not the most immediate means to union with God; the practice of theological virtues and participation in the sacraments is much more efficacious.

But there comes a stage when the thinking of the church leaders becomes too abstract, too remote from the day-to-day life of a lay person. It is at this point that cults and counter-movements spring up, argues Bryan Wilson. Each of these at first offers a re-interpretation of the central doctrines of Christianity in ways that are more comprehensible to the layman, that offer a more direct line to God. More established churches may also, in reaction, re-define their direction. But as Elaine Pagels, in her book called *The Gnostic Gospels*, points out the established church cannot survive on a diet of Gnosticism alone. If the early Christian church had totally swung over to the Gnostic position, she observes, it is doubtful whether it would have survived. Thus a possible interpretation of the broad sweep of church history could be a see-saw between an intellectual, rational approach, and an intuitive, personal, mystical approach. The Marian manifestations can be interpreted as the beginnings of a possible swing to the intuitive side of the expression of our faith.

The charismatic 'born again' movement has many of the elements of the Gnostic tradition, even if its members would regard the original documents of the so-called 'Gnostic Gospels' with grave suspicion. There are many other contemporary cults and beliefs which have sprung up on the fringes of Christianity which also stress the possibility of the ordinary person having this direct knowledge of his God.

It is tempting to put the Marian apparitions into this sort of context. They could be seen as expressions of the deep-rooted religious feelings of the mass of Irish people in the face of a Catholic church which has gradually got rid of a lot of its mystical trappings. Many Catholic commentators have spoken about the gradual 'Protestantisation' of the Roman Catholic faith since the Second Vatican Council.

In Garabandal, in Spain, Our Lady appeared to four girls,

who, at the time of the first appearance, were between the ages of eleven and twelve. Garabandal has been categorically dismissed by the Catholic church, but many of the 'messages' received by the girls from Our Lady spoke about her concern with the decline in standards in the church and the coming of a retribution. I have seen a number of pamphlets unofficially circulated by Roman Catholics which dwell on the implications of the Garabandal apparitions. These pamphlets are emphatically not approved of by the Roman Catholic church, and they attribute the decline to the outcomes of the Second Vatican Council.

It is tempting to see the popularity of the Marian apparitions as part of the same process; what one might call a 'fundamentalist Roman Catholic backlash'.

A few weeks ago, I would have been very hesitant to express these ideas in public. I am, after all, not a theologian nor am I an expert on Irish Catholicism. The Bishop of Cork gave a recorded interview which was broadcast on the BBC Radio 4 religious affairs programme called *Soundings* on Saturday 28 September 1985. His remarks went a lot further than I would have done, but then, he *is* an expert in these matters.

He spoke of the Ballinspittle phenomenon as a form of popular devotion that has been missing in Catholicism, and whose lack has been felt. The growth of the intellectual approach in Catholicism, he went on, since the Second Vatican Council, has passed over the heads of the people. There has been little attempt, he pointed out, to promote a genuine lay spirituality in the church. Such attempts as there have been have had their origins in Spain or have been Spanish-orientated. We should be able to find a tradition that is specially Irish from the rich resources that we have. Many of these resources have been lost for hundreds of years, but now is the time to start to work out a tradition that combines a recognition of God's presence among people and things with a devotion to the scriptures.

Many of the letters I read echoed these sentiments before Bishop Murphy had uttered them, although nobody was as critical of the effect of the Second Vatical Council as he. An old lady I had known many years ago was part of a group that met on a weekly basis to say the rosary in church. She spoke to me often with some sadness about the falling away from devotion to Our Lady that she saw in the modern church. She also said that she thought privately that the Second Vatican Council had maybe made some wrong decisions, but she and millions of other Catholics had faith in their clergy. 'I'm just an old woman,' she would tell me. 'I guess it's not easy for me to change.'

I have presented three main theories about the rise of the Marian apparitions, and tried to relate them to what has been said about them. Social anthropology is not an experimental science like psychology. If these theories sound speculative, they are nevertheless also highly appealing to the intuition. Each in its own right has captured some element of what seems to have been going on this summer. Perhaps the full explanation of 'why' can be found in a combination of all three: suddenly, this summer, a combination of the economic, the social, and the religious had come together in Ireland to produce a massive and unheard-of social phenomenon.

Inasmuch as we can fathom the often inscrutable ways of God, He seems to prefer to use natural means to give us His messages. St Thomas Aquinas wrote, 'God moves all things according to their nature.' If, therefore, you wish to believe that He has spoken directly to many of His people this summer, this does not mean that you must reject the scientific explanations of the past few chapters. What would be more natural than for Himself to use the laws of nature He has created?

On the other hand, if you are sceptical about the whole thing, then I hope the explanations I have offered have at least given you an alternative to the seventeenth century Scottish philosopher David Hume's scathing dismissal. In his *Enquiry concerning Human Understanding* he wrote:

> It forms a strong presumption against all supernatural and miraculous relations, that they are observed chiefly to

abound among ignorant and barbarous nations.

People who have neither religious faith nor an interest in science have indeed doomed themselves to a life of ignorance and barbarism.

Epilogue: Prudence and Caution

The Catholic church authorities are in no hurry to investigate the happenings at the grotto in Ballinspittle. 'Privately,' said a BBC 2 report, 'the local Bishop would be more than happy to see the whole thing fade away but since the church believes in miracles the bishop can hardly say this one is impossible, merely that it is unlikely.'

The church was very slow even to make any kind of statement. The local parish priest, Fr Neville, and the curate, Fr Davern, not only did not take any apparent interest in the happenings, they did not once mention them during the homily at Sunday mass – even though in excess of a quarter of a million people had made their way to the grotto, half a mile down the road. As in such cases official comment was left to the Bishop of Cork and Ross, Dr Michael Murphy. The bishop has not visited the shrine himself. 'I feel that if I went down it might be a signal that I was promoting it perhaps.'

On the evening of 30 July the bishop's press officer, Fr Diarmuid Lenihan, released the following statement from Dr Murphy:

> Direct supernatural intervention is a very rare happening in life, so common sense would demand that we approach the claims made concerning the grotto at Ballinspittle with prudence and caution. Before any definite pronouncement could be made by the church, all natural explanations would have to be examined and exhausted over a lengthy period of time.
>
> In instances of this kind one has to be extremely careful not to raise expectations unduly.
>
> I understand that crowds are gathering there in a great spirit of prayer. This is certainly a praise-worthy thing. It is in keeping with the devotion and respect that is expected

at all shrines.

For many the pronouncement which had been eagerly awaited proved disappointing but it did show at least that the church was keeping an open mind. Since July the bishop has only made one further pronouncement but he has not yet set in train any official investigation. In a letter to the papers in September Bishop Thomas McDonnell of Killala referred to the autokinetic theory dealt with elsewhere in this book (see chapter 4). But the questions posed by Ballinspittle and some thirty other shrines around the country are grave indeed for the church. The Augustinian theologian Fr Gabriel Daly tackled the issue bluntly in the *Sunday Independent*: 'The question that has been nagging at my mind is far from disdaining or patronising. Where are we – pastors and teachers alike – failing in our presentation of the good news, when people have to turn to moving statues in order to satisfy their spiritual needs?' In ways it is as though the people wish to return to a pre-Second Vatican Council church with its ritual, Latin mass – and its statues. Fr Daly wrote:

> The scene at Ballinspittle is a replica of old-style evening devotions that not so long ago could be seen in churches up and down the country. The main difference was that here the congregation was in the open air and behaved rather more informally than it would in church. The prayers, the hymns, the manner of recitation were the same. Here, of course, unlike the evening devotions, there was an atmosphere of expectation that something extraordinary might happen.

Though the Second Vatican Council introduced a wide range of reforms in the theology of Our Lady it appears to have had very little practical effect on popular Marian devotion.

An *Irish Times* journalist Mary Holland also pinpointed the nature of the problem for the church, the problem of how to give spiritual leadership to a church which has become quite 'schizoid' in character. 'How in fact, can they cater for those who go to Ballinspittle and those who, in Peter Prendergast's words, are "laughing heartily" at it. Since the Second Vatican Council, though by no means entirely because of it, the Catholic church in Ireland has in the main come to terms with the fact that it can no longer exercise the old, unquestioned authority over its flock.'

Ms Holland continued:

> Half the population is under twenty-five and subject to far too many influences over which the bishops have no control. In any case, many of their parents have already refused to accept the church's teachings on such matters as contraception, the indissolubility of marriage or even what is or isn't a mortal sin. The liberal establishment, which may be small but is tiresomely vocal, keeps on and on about pluralism, the separation of church and state, the need to be more generous to Protestants, particularly if the ghastly problems of the North are ever to be resolved.
>
> If all the movement was in one direction, as it has been in some European countries, it would be easier in some ways for the hierarchy to resolve its problems, at least at a purely pragmatic level. Mass in the vernacular, folk songs instead of Benediction, priests leading demonstrations against President Reagan's foreign policy, a lot of concern about social issues, all these would go a long way towards easing the transition between the old pre-Vatican Two authority and a new more equal relationship between priests and people.
>
> But, as Ballinspittle illustrates, very many Irish Catholics want nothing to do with the new enlightenment and are deeply fearful of the intellectual challenges it presents. They yearn for the old rituals – the Latin Mass, the family rosary which provided a focus for the evening to which errant children could be summoned, the votive lamp flickering before the statue of the Sacred Heart. It's easy to scoff but these things gave a warmth and comfort to their faith which the new colder ceremonies have failed to

> replace, just as the absolute moral authority of the bishops gave a shape and certainty to their lives, now and in the hereafter.

There is a great deal of interest at the attitude of the church particularly in their apparent belief that there is a wholly rational explanation. It is obviously anxious on the one hand to encourage communal prayer but on the other entirely condemns idolatry. 'Does its (the church's) reluctance to engage in the scientific observation of the reported phenomenon stem from a desire to see collective prayer even at some cost to truth, many of us ask ourselves?' wrote a *Cork Examiner* reporter, Pat Casey, in a previously mentioned article.

The church has given, it is true, too little attention to the role of the imagination in religion. Much of the art and sculpture is sentimental and plain, almost ugly. Yet it is upon this that the imagination of the flock feeds. Former professor of moral theology at Maynooth College and currently parish priest of Mallow, Canon Denis O'Callaghan has written extensively on the church's view on apparitions. He is very much aware of the 'epidemic' nature of these so-called apparitions. Even Lourdes, he argues, experienced this. Writing in *The Kerryman* he said:

> The vision of Our Lady to Bernadette was followed by a whole series of parallel claims from neighbouring areas. The apparitions at Beauraing and Banneux in Belgium during 1232-33 were followed by at least a dozen alleged apparitions of similar type. In these cycles there is a marked 'mimetic' quality in the claims – signs on the sun, showers of flower petals, aromas of sweet perfume – drawing on reports of occurrences during earlier often authentic apparitions.

A multiple of parallel claims, he said, often delays official church sanction. 'You will admit the need for prudence when you appreciate that for the period 1928-1971 specialists in Marian devotion have listed 232 claims of apparitions of Our

Lady to which the church has not extended any recognition.' The canon pointed out that if and when the church does pronounce a negative decision it may be very definite and include a total prohibition of pilgrimages and devotions. This has happened in the case of Garabandal and Palmar de Troya.

> These have attracted the most unambiguous condemnation including interdiction of all liturgical acts, suspension of priests who celebrate any ceremony and excommunication of those ordained by schismatic bishops. Normally, however, the decision is much less severe.
>
> The majority of apparitions and other allegedly miraculous phenomena have failed to gain recognition either because fraud has been proved or suspected or because the possibility of hallucination and hysteria cannot be ruled out. In fact in any supposedly preternatural phenomenon the presumption is that it is due to one or other of these factors. . .
>
> Fraud or deliberate deception on the part of the self-styled visionary does not usually get very far. The character of the subject and the questionable nature of the circumstances betray what is afoot.

Canon O'Callaghan points out that hallucination is a more common explanation. Here there is no attempt to deceive. Indeed it is the would-be visionaries themselves who are totally deceived. They have no motive to use deception of any kind.

Another common explanation is 'group hysteria' where people confirm each other's visions. Again sincerity and conviction are not at stake. It is truth and honesty which are.

The procedure adopted by the church is that if visions persist over a period of time, the local bishop sets up a commission to investigate. The commission will look very hard at the circumstances. Canon O'Callaghan again:

> First the message itself. Is it bizarre or self-contradictory? Is it stressing some marginal practice rather than the essentials of Christian living? Is it full of threats of apocalyptic doom and gloom unless some devotion is performed?
>
> Second the visionary: Is there genuine sincerity and humility? Is there an absence of self-interest and exaggeration? Is the day-to-day life that of someone who is living a Christian faith?
>
> Third, the concerned third parties. Do they show real humility and respect for Christ and His saints? Do they show obedience to Church guidance? Are they discreet and disinterested?
>
> Fourth, the crowds. Does the apparition move them to prayer and to live the Christian life more seriously? Are they happy and peaceful rather than fanatical? Is it curiosity for the sensational and emotional which attracts them?

If after exhaustive enquiries the church is satisfied that a case can be made for a genuine apparition, a report is sent to the Congregation of the Faith in the Vatican who may or may not make a decision.

> The church [says Canon O'Callaghan] is very aware that hysterical personalities are attracted to any cause or movement that stresses emotional or religious experience. She knows how suggestible young people are. She is concerned about the harm that these people can do themselves and others by going 'over the top' or putting others 'over the top' or by simply leading to dead ends and empty distractions.
>
> Any religious phenomenon or experience can only be marginal to gospel faith. If it deepens that faith, it may well be from God. If it distracts from it, it certainly cannot be from Him. The acid test frequently is: Do these experiences make for genuine Christian life? We have the Lord's own words: 'You will be able to tell them by their fruits.' (Matthew 7:6)

The Catholic church has always endorsed external aids to prayer, as she recognises that it is difficult for most people to concentrate on God in the abstract. Statues and holy shrines are important because they help us get nearer to God but they are never ends in themselves. Irish society has always had a place for the supernatural and this tradition lives strongest in rural areas such as Ballinspittle. Irish society also has a strong devotion to Our Lady. Mary and the saints 'pray for us' but they don't act directly. Mary, as the mother of Christ, has a special influence and intercedes on behalf of those who ask for help. There are many delicate dividing lines and the church is always trying to keep these lines clear. As Father Gabriel Daly wrote:

> There is a great deal to be said for the spiritual value of holy places. We Irish have a long tradition of devotion to them. They give localised expression to the presence of God's grace which is everywhere. But they also show how thin is the line which separates faith from superstition and grace from magic. Failure in respect for that line can easily put a frivolous idol in the place of a holy God.

Finally, a word from well-known Dublin priest, Fr Fergal O'Connor. Writing in the *Irish Independent* he again re-echoed the thoughts of Fr Daly and Mary Holland by arguing that there is 'evidence that we are turning back into the supposed darkness of the Middle Ages'.

> Suddenly something as irrational as a moving statue shatters the dreams of the 'enlightened' and challenges their theories, and they are unable to cope with it. . . According to their picture of life there is a relevant skill for solving all our problems, if only we get enough people who possess it out into the field. . . And various problems like unwanted pregnancies, unhappy marriages, unemployment, crimes, etc. would all disappear. Sadly man does not live by knowledge alone. Human problems are not solved by skilled operators. Perhaps these recent events

may at least help us to see the kind of vision of human life to which we are unconsciously subscribing.

Time alone will test Ballinspittle, as it has all other holy places. And the test will not be proving whether the statue moved or not, but whether men and women, even if only a few, will continue to find God there, and draw closer to Him in their daily lives. These events won't cause any unwanted pregnancies, or cause people to reject the unmarried mother. Conceivably, but not likely they might help us question a lot of unjust practices which follow from our enlightened theories.

The Power of Charismatic Healing

A Personal Account

Andy O'Neill

The Power of Charismatic Healing deals specifically with healing by the laying on of hands. It is the story of Andy O'Neill's personal experience of healing in this manner.

Healing by the laying on of hands is relevant and important today and it will shock the majority of readers. *The Power of Charismatic Healing* will challenge a whole host of non-believers with its rational business-like approach. It is a book which has not been written by a mystic, a visionary or a priest. It was written by a businessman who lives in, and enjoys, today's world.

Atheists, agnostics and people of other beliefs may question or reject the basis of the Charismatic Renewal Movement and its healing ministry – the Christian faith – but the happenings described in this book, which range from the simple to the incredible, cannot be denied. All of these events happened before Andy O'Neill's eyes and the presence of others. By any standards this is a great, true story.

The God I Don't Believe In

Juan Arias

The modern world, it is clear, has gradually developed a completely different approach to God and the Supernatural. We no longer think of Divine Providence riding the clouds in the distant heavens, but as a Father understandable in human terms: warm, accessible, non-authoritarian – a God for all men who have grown weary of the ancient image of an implacable Jehovah.

This 'new' and 'credible' God is the subject of this book – a book which will make, in its warmth and feeling, immediate contact with the reader.

'A real joy; something superb. One must only read it; and then let his heart speak' – *Fruili* (Italian).

Already in Italian, French, German, Portuguese – and now in English, *The God I Don't Believe In* is addressed – with gusto – to all contemporary Christians.